"Elaine Holland has done a terrific job in this book. It is an 'easy read' by design, but without sacrificing depth. Drawing from her broad business experience and a lifetime of captivating anecdotes, she teaches leaders how to humanize today's workplace. I can attest she knows her stuff!"

— Bob Meyers, retired CEO of Millward Brown

"In this book, Elaine writes like she talks: conversational, interesting, to the point, and easy to understand. I've read many business and life-help books over a 43 year career, and this is one of the best I've ever read. It has down-to-earth lessons and real life experiences we can all learn from."

— Coby Sillers, retired VP at Cox Communications

LEADING
FOR THE
LONG RUN

STORIES AND INSIGHTS FROM
A LIFETIME IN BUSINESS

LEADING
FOR THE
LONG RUN

STORIES AND INSIGHTS FROM
A LIFETIME IN BUSINESS

ELAINE HOLLAND

ISBN 979-8-9933333-0-4 (paperback)
ISBN 979-8-9933333-1-1 (eBook)

Published by Holland Publishing

Book Design: Molly Seabrook, Credible Ink

First Edition 2025

Printed in the United States of America

I dedicate this book to business owners, managers and employees.
May the stories, insights and wisdom help illuminate your path,
especially during difficult times.

If you have knowledge, let others light their candles in it.

– Margaret Fuller

Contents

INTRODUCTION

"That was the worst presentation I have ever seen"

In the late 1990s, I found myself standing in front of the board of directors of a New York bank making a presentation intended to clinch a major deal for technology services.

The deal was important enough for me to feel some pressure, but I felt ready for the moment. More than two decades into a career by then, I had delivered countless presentations to prospects, clients, and colleagues. Although this one fell in the "bigger and more pressure" category, I was no rookie.

Oh... and I should also mention that my boss Ross Perot was in the room.

Ross Perot's name might not be immediately familiar to those of a certain age, but back then he was extremely well-known. Perot was the multi-billionaire founder of two highly successful companies, Electronic Data Systems, and then Perot Systems (the company where I worked at the time).

Ross also ran for president in 1992 as an independent and received a substantial number of votes. All this added up to him being famous and successful, and he had a reputation as a straight talker and someone with strong beliefs about how things should be done.

I had met him face-to-face once before to talk about this deal. Our interaction had gone well. So despite the demands of the situation, I felt reasonably confident.

My team dimmed the lights, and I walked the board through my carefully prepared and rehearsed PowerPoint presentation. When it was over, I felt everything had gone well.

As the owner of Perot Systems, Ross was there to assure the board that he was involved with the deal and that they were making a safe decision. At the end of the presentation, the lights were turned up and Ross fielded questions from the board members and that was that.

With the presentation over, we left so the board could discuss the deal on their own. Our team retreated to a meeting room the board had provided us for what I thought would be a positive recap of the presentation.

A few steps into the room, Ross turned directly to me, and in that somewhat harsh, Texas-inflected, nasal twang of his, said:

"That was the worst presentation I have ever seen."

OUCH.

Actually, ouch does not begin to cover it. It is the kind of moment that makes you want to cry or crawl into a hole or throw something. Or maybe all three.

Instead, I quickly recovered from the initial shock and opened the presentation on my laptop. And then in a calm voice, I said, "Okay, let's go through it. What specifically didn't you like about it?"

"It was too dark in that room, you can't see the reactions of the people," Ross said. I realized that was true. The whole point of any presentation or similar communication is to connect with the people you are trying to persuade in a genuine way. If I couldn't see reactions, how could I know if or how the message was being received?

Next, he started going through the presentation. He pointed out that the print on the slides was too small. Again, I could immediately see he had a point. And part of the reason the print was too small was because many of the slides were jammed with too much detail.

Ross definitely noticed that, too. He asked questions like, "What's the key point of this slide?" adding, "this slide is too confusing." He got to about the fifth slide before his frustration boiled over and he slammed the laptop shut. And then he left.

This story has a funny ending (and, I should add, a happy ending in that we did win the contract from the bank).

But before I get to the humor, I want to share what went through my head as I reeled from the news that I had just delivered the worst presentation Ross Perot had ever seen.

At that moment, I managed to hold this thought in my mind: "Don't cry, get curious." In those few seconds, I repeated that phrase several times in my head. I also instinctively knew from years of sales and leadership that in a moment of extreme adversity, I needed to switch the focus from me and my emotions, and get the focus back on him.

Instead of dwelling on my feelings, I asked for specifics about what he didn't like. That in turn gave me valuable information about what could be improved. And while Ross's feedback may come across as rough handling, I will take this kind of honesty over dull platitudes any day.

There is a beauty in being told the truth straight up, and if you want to play in the biggest moments with highly successful people, you have to be able to handle it.

Of course, that does not mean I wasn't still reeling in the moment. After a blow like that, it feels like everything is on the table. Was I about to get fired?

I held my breath when later that day, the director of my department at Perot Systems, called.

"Well," he said. "I already got a call from Ross on his plane. He always complains about two things in every meeting. One, that the presentation was terrible. And, two, that there are too many of his people in the room – he always wants them to be somewhere else using their time productively. Congratulations Elaine, he only complained about the presentation."

"So, you mean I'm not going to be fired?" I said, only half-jokingly at that point.

"No Elaine, you're not going to get fired," he said.

It was a nice use of humor from a leader in the moment, and also an actual relief!

Why I Wrote This Book and Who It Can Help

I have been amazingly fortunate in my 50-year career. (Although, as we'll cover later, luck is something you have to be ready for, too).

My first big career step was being one of the first women IBM hired as a salesperson. It was an exceptional culture in which to learn and grow. And my final career stop was as Director of Coaching for another amazing organization, Robbins Research International, founded by Tony Robbins, the man who created the coaching industry.

In between, there were lots of other remarkable companies and roles. Looking back, I feel tremendous gratitude, and that thankfulness is the driving motivation for writing this book. In many ways, I think of it as a long thank you note to the people, experiences, and authors that have impacted my journey.

Gratitude naturally leads to another motivation: to pass it on to others. Five decades worth of successes, adversities, and stories teach many lessons and bring a lot of insights. Advice that has been battle-tested and full of practical application is the best kind of all. What I share here is exactly that.

The stories and insights can help if any of these describe you:

- You are at or near the starting gate of a life in business. You have a fire inside you to create a long, successful career. There is a way to build that kind of life with intention, and the stories and lessons that can make it happen are in this book.

- You are new to a leadership role or are in a mid-level position and feel stuck. The higher you climb, the more insight you need. If you are overwhelmed in a new role, or are feeling trapped in an old one, this book can be a reliable source of wisdom to guide you forward.

- You are a business owner or CEO who found early success but growing pains or downturns in your business are causing you pain or making you uneasy. Are you being a true leader? Are there ways you could empower yourself more and get the most out of your people? This book can reveal a path forward.

There will be many lessons in the chapters to follow, and they will address very practical situations and give you specific strategies proven to work.

However, as we dig into the details of what works, certain themes emerge again and again.

As a business leader or owner, to grow means to increasingly master your grasp of these themes and implement them. Here's a brief overview of the fundamental insights:

LESS IS MORE

A key leadership skill is learning to distill things down to essentials. For example, in Chapter 3, I'll tell you about a boss of mine who once said, "Learn to stop talking before I stop listening." He was telling me very concisely that I needed to be more succinct and thoughtful in my own communication.

Or, to pick another example, in Chapter 10 I discuss a simple but extremely powerful definition of culture. Across all kinds of situations described in this book, you will see this theme again and again: less is almost always more.

LEARN TO ANTICIPATE

Here's a good example of how to anticipate: If you have a presentation coming up in front of an executive team or a prospective client, ask yourself, "What question do I hope they won't ask?" Then figure out your answer to that question.

Or let's say you are in a role where you regularly outline proposals and potential solutions for your bosses or your customers. Are you tracking their responses and looking for patterns, and then using that information to become even better at recommending solutions and proposals? You should be. (See Chapter 4 for more on this).

The point is: mediocre leaders rarely go the extra step of intentionally anticipating anything beyond standard expectations. To be great, you need to be the person who anticipates. It doesn't take special clairvoyance; it just takes hard work.

In all kinds of situations throughout this book, you will see that great leaders anticipate, and it pays off.

BE SPECIFIC

I wrote a book several years ago called Making Feedback Work. The most fundamental point in the book is that most feedback is way too vague, and that includes both positive and negative feedback. In this book, we'll go deeper on the thought process behind great feedback. Once you see how it works, it will transform how you see the world. You'll start seeing everything through this filter.

But being specific and detailed goes beyond feedback. When I first arrived at Perot Systems, I was asked to find out why the company had just lost out on a billion-dollar contract. The answer was in the details, a lesson and story I share in Chapter 12.

If you fear financial numbers, you are not alone. But learning to handle and understand specific numbers is important, and is also not as hard as you think. It requires only that you are willing to dig into details to understand the connection between specific tasks and the impact on the bottom line.

In short, getting specific matters, and great leaders know that

REFUSE TO BE A VICTIM

This might be the best leadership (and life) advice of all: refuse to see yourself as a victim.

It's true that unlucky and unfair things will happen to you. And, yes, sometimes people will let you down, or even betray you. You will want to throw a pity party for yourself (and this is even allowed, but with an important rule to keep it from getting out of hand – Chapter 9 will explain).

But there will be other times when you think you are being treated unfairly, when in fact you are the problem, or at least a good bit of it. Later in this book, you'll learn how your judgment of others may actually reveal more about you than them. Once you get this, it can completely transform how you approach a problem with a boss, colleague, or team member.

Whatever the situation, make a radical commitment to never be a victim. Reject victimhood no matter what, and shift to always taking responsibility for your actions, results, and feelings.

It is not my intent to say that all the lessons in this book can be grouped under these four categories – not by a long shot. There's lots of insights in here (50 years is a long time to accumulate some battle-tested wisdom!). But as you begin this journey, it is helpful to watch for these key patterns that go into the making of a seasoned leader.

How to Get the Most Out of This Book

There are three key tools to help you to squeeze the most value out of this book.

28 LESSONS

In each chapter, you'll find 'Lesson Boxes' (look for the Lightbulb Icon). These highlight the book's key takeaways. It is a little like having notes taken for you. This will allow you to skim back through at any time to find something immediately useful when faced with a particular issue.

You could also keep the book handy on a bedside table or at your desk and crack it open regularly to find and study a key insight when you can snatch five minutes of time. Great leaders become that way because they continually look for ways to grow their skills. My hope is that this book can serve any reader who is passionate about self-improvement.

BOOK RECOMMENDATIONS

Over the course of my career, I have found several books that have proved transformative. These titles and authors are shared throughout. Of course, I do this to give credit where credit is due. But more so, I hope you will seek out these books and let them transform you as they did me.

If you find a certain chapter resonating with you, go deeper by finding the book referred to and increase your mastery even more.

Note: You will also find a complete list of books referenced in the text in the 'Recommended Reading' Appendix.

BRINGING IT ALL TOGETHER

In Chapter 19, all 28 Lessons come together for your reference. This way if you are struggling or simply need some inspiration, you can quickly skim the lessons and remind yourself of where to go in the book for a problem you are currently facing.

There are additional lists in that final chapter where lessons are broken out by topic. For example, if you are struggling with some aspect of your career development, go to the Career Development lessons list and review it. What ones might help you right now? The hope is that this will make it easy to use the concepts in the book at the time when you most need them.

In addition to these three tools, please enjoy the stories. While meant to be entertaining, they have a deeper purpose: I want to "put you there." Sometimes you will see me messing up because failure is more interesting than success. Sometimes you will see me escaping with some quick thinking, sometimes you will see me working hard to make sure I anticipate a problem before it happens, as well as many other situations.

Ask yourself how these stories relate to your own business choices. Certainly your circumstances will differ in the details, but surely you will have found yourself in some comparable situations or facing similar challenges. Visualizing the story and knowing the details should help you see better ways to move forward and find more success.

At the bottom of all of this, that's my hope and wish for you: that the lessons and insights—while costing me some pain, sweat, and tears—will allow you to jump forward faster and better. I also want you to see how much fun it was building a career, and how many excellent people you can meet along your journey.

So let's be on our way.

And, as is appropriate for Chapter 1, we'll begin at the beginning. It all started when I learned that as a trained art historian, I made a pretty good waitress…

LUCK, PERSISTENCE, AND OPPORTUNITY

I was set up beautifully for a great start to my career.

And, wow, was I miserable.

Having just graduated as an art history major from Goucher College, an excellent liberal arts school in Baltimore, I was ready to apply what I had learned over the past four years to grow a successful career.

I landed a job at a museum, working with an art restorer. This should have been perfect, as I also had minored in chemistry, which gave me some knowledge of the materials used in restoration. Obviously I still had much to learn, but the job seemed an ideal match to my educational background and skills.

So there I was, all day in a room with just me and the painting I was restoring. And, oh my, was I ever bored. No one to talk to or laugh with. No one to create with or join forces to do something purposeful.

Since entry-level arts jobs don't pay much, and living in an urban area on the East Coast wasn't cheap, I also waitressed at night.

And I LOVED being a waitress. I formed relationships with the regular patrons, remembering what they liked, asking them about family, and simply enjoying the human-to-human connection. Money from tips wasn't bad either, but it was the sociability and vibe of the restaurant that perfectly matched my personality.

I did love art history – and still do to this day – but actual day-to-day work as a restorer didn't fit my extrovert personality. I needed the oxygen of other people.

That left me with a decision to make. Should I continue doing work that bored me to tears or find a better path forward? Seen from one perspective, it would seem almost insane to stick with a job I knew wasn't a fit. But how many people DO stay way too long, sometimes a lifetime, doing something they can't stand because it's too painful to admit the plan isn't working?

How many people keep plodding along no matter what, because change feels too scary or embarrassing? And it's not just your internal feelings, either. It's hard to own up how you feel to family, friends, and colleagues.

You can imagine the courage it took for me to call my parents and essentially say, "You just paid for four years of college… and, oh by the way, I love being a waitress."

The turning point, which I remember to this day, came while riding a bus from the museum to the restaurant. I was in a meditative frame of mind, the half-dreamy state you can get on a bus or a train. My internal voice came through loud and clear: "This isn't working." It was not that I was being a quitter because something was too hard or challenging. My inner voice was whispering to me that what I was doing was not a match with who I was.

If that meant throwing away the value of a four-year degree, so be it. (Of course, it did not turn out to be a waste at all). It was time to reassess.

LESSON #1: HAVE THE COURAGE TO CHANGE

When you know in your heart "this isn't working," be brave enough to make a change.

This may sound almost too simple to be a lesson, but I have seen many people struggle to slow down enough to listen to their inner promptings and suffer as a result.

You cannot let fear of the unknown, attachment to comfort, or worry about what others might think keep you stuck.

Related: Later, I'll discuss big career disruptions that happen to almost everyone at one point or another. You'll learn about the "whispers of destiny" and not being afraid of the "neutral zone." See Chapter 17.

Ultimately, I decided to return to Oregon where I grew up and began working for a place called the Oregon Marketing Exchange. One day a potential customer named Coby Sillers walked in, and it was my good fortune to be assigned to him. It would be a life-changing encounter.

After chatting with Coby for about ten minutes, he asked, "Do you have a college degree?" Thanks to my time at Goucher College, I sure did.

Coby then asked if I would consider applying for a sales position with International Business Machines Corporation – better known as IBM, where Coby worked.

Of course, all these years later IBM is still a well-recognized and respected name. But back then, it was especially considered a "cream of the crop" organization with which anyone would love to be associated. Nicknamed Big Blue, IBM was founded in 1911 as the Computing-Tabulating-Recording Company and over time it became the kind of place where you could build a successful career. So, yes, you could say I was interested!

Coby explained that IBM wanted to increase the number of women in their sales division. This was the mid 1970s, and companies were waking up to the fact that society was changing and they needed to change, too. The number of women in sales was near zero at the time. (Interestingly, there was at least a little more female presence on the technical side at IBM; the book and movie Hidden Figures showed this same phenomenon at NASA).

I'll never be 100 percent sure of what Coby saw from such a short chat to suggest that I apply, but I think I had four things going for me:

- I could talk to anybody. It's something that comes naturally. I've always acted on the belief that a stranger is just a friend I haven't met yet.

- The Oregon Marketing Exchange taught me proven sales skills. There really was no choice, because we were maybe one step up from the door-to-door vacuum cleaner salesperson. I think Coby picked up on my training and could sense that I had worked hard to master the skills.

- As noted, IBM wanted to hire more women.

- I had a college diploma. It didn't matter that I didn't have a business or finance degree; my diploma was my entry ticket to apply to IBM. Had I skipped college and gone straight to waitressing or selling at the Oregon Marketing Exchange, I would have been disqualified before I even started.

Note that the "grace of time" played in here, too. When I left the Baltimore area after resigning from my art restoration gig, I questioned whether my degree would ever be of value to me. After my conversation with Coby, I was certainly glad I had it.

THE VALUE OF A COLLEGE DEGREE

In recent years some people have begun to argue that going to college doesn't offer much value. I would argue the opposite: college is still one of the best ways to invest in developing yourself.

Even though I studied art history and not business, getting my liberal arts education gave me skills that fundamentally contributed to my business success. My ability to think logically, do research, write clearly, and meet deadlines is all rooted in my time at Goucher.

I remember vividly getting back my first writing assignment at college and staring at a "D" at the top of the paper. I was a 4.0 student in high school, so it shocked me. But it also made me realize that I needed to step up my game to a whole new level.

Fortunately, one of my friends went through the paper with me to help me understand what I needed to do to improve my grade. At Goucher, the expectation was for original thought, not just reporting on what others have said. And those thoughts had to be logically presented. Learning how to research, think and write clearly helped my career even if the content of what I learned wasn't directly relevant to a business career.

If you happen to be a young person reading this, my advice is to go to college and use that time well.

Anyway, I got my interview with IBM and then… they hired someone else.

Not what I was hoping for obviously, but I asked Coby to meet for coffee. When we got together, the question I did *not* ask was: "Why didn't I get hired?"

Instead, my two main questions were:

- What can I do next time to improve?
- What did the candidate who was hired have that I did not?

The answer to both questions came down to the same thing. I had sales skills, but I did not understand the language of business and finance. As an IBM salesperson, I would be talking with business owners and I would need to be able to speak this language.

The candidate IBM hired had a degree in finance, which gave him the edge over my art history degree. After processing this feedback, my next question was, "What is the basic information I need to be able to communicate with the business owner?"

Keep in mind that this was way, way before the internet and search engines. It was not nearly so easy to access information as it is now. I still remember Coby handing me a red folder that contained a pamphlet called "How to Read a Balance Sheet." I guess we could call that red folder the Google results of the mid 1970s!

I read the pamphlet, took the time to digest and understand it, and in the second interview I could speak the language of business much more fluently.

And once again, I was rejected in favor of another candidate.

At this point, I was tempted to file this experience under the category of "not meant to be." But I wasn't quite ready to let this opportunity go. I summoned the willpower and courage to call Coby to meet again for coffee.

This time I asked if maybe an art history degree was too much of a barrier for IBM to take my candidacy seriously. Coby encouraged me not to give up. "You just need to be persistent."

He was right. Throughout the process, I had already learned a lot about both IBM and business language. The next interview would be an opportunity to show that I was determined and relentless.

After the third interview, I got a phone call telling me I was hired. Of course I was incredibly excited. Joining a prestigious company represented a giant step forward from the Oregon Marketing Exchange. But I also felt a little like the proverbial dog that caught the car.

As persistent as I had been, I had begun to let the thought creep in that I would never catch that car. But now, here I was being told that it actually happened. The mind races: "Oh my gosh, what do I do now? What have I got myself into?"

One funny postscript to this whole story gives a window into a different time. After hearing I was hired, I had a practical problem to solve immediately, and that was to have something appropriate to wear for my new role.

I walked into a Nordstrom in Portland, Oregon and said, "I just got hired by IBM. I need to dress like a businessperson. Can you help me?" The look on the salesperson's face told me she didn't have a clue on how to help me. Back then, men wore suits, white shirts and ties at IBM. For them, knowing how to look professional at the office was straightforward. Dressing up for women usually meant dinner dresses, and that would not work at the office!

We did manage to get some outfits together that would get the job done. It wasn't until 1988 when Nordstrom formed an exclusive distribution partnership with Faconnable that women were able to buy fashionable business attire.

The other thing I did upon being hired was to quietly set myself a goal to outsell the two people hired ahead of me. This was not about "proving" IBM wrong about overlooking me twice. This was not about revenge. It was about setting the highest standards and benchmarks for myself. It was less about beating out others and more about pushing myself to add the most value I could.

LESSON #2: THE RIGHT RESPONSE TO A SETBACK IS "WHAT CAN I DO TO IMPROVE?"

You may not get a job or a promotion you were up for. You may have a business plan that derailed from circumstances that were hard to foresee. Whatever the setback, don't blame the system, or the hiring person, or think it's because you have the wrong degree. This also includes blaming the business climate, or any other reasons you can come up with.

Even if the reasons you could come up with had some validity, it is a waste of your time to dwell on external forces. That kind of focus will not help you get where you want to go.

Focus on two simple things instead: One, do not look for reasons you cannot control. And two, ask what you can do to improve, and what are the practical actions you can take to make that improvement. Don't dwell on anything else.

Related: Later in the book I'll discuss a concept called "Be the Board" that makes a similar point in a different way. See Lesson #9.

CHAPTER 2

THE RIGHT WORDS AT THE RIGHT TIME

Things got off to a good start at IBM. I met my goal of outperforming my new colleagues. Of course, having the best products in the industry, and a good command of why they were superior, made selling easier.

While being one of the first woman salespeople had some disadvantages, there were upsides, too. Being a woman in technology sales – which made me a bit of a unicorn – sometimes helped get in the door with business owners.

At times it also worked against me. That's because after the initial interest, some prospective male clients preferred to take things to the next step with another male. Still, as a salesperson, whatever helps you get in the door is a good start. Over time I learned that bringing my male product specialists or marketing manager added "credibility" when closing a significant order. It wasn't fair, but that's what was required at the time.

I also learned the importance of listening carefully to what prospective clients were telling me and knowing when to shift to another of IBM's products rather than the one I was trying to sell. For instance, after hearing a business owner tell me for the third time he did not need a new word processing system, I knew it was time to pivot.

"You know," I told him, "when I really look at it, I see your point. Your current word processing system works fine for your needs. So investing in an upgrade probably won't be cost effective for you. But I couldn't help but notice your dictation equipment is at least 15 years old, and the technology available today is so much better. If I were you, that is what I would invest in."

"Okay," he said. "Show me that."

I grabbed the latest version of the IBM dictation system from my car, and a few minutes later, I got the sale..

LESSON #3: PERSISTENCE IS GOOD, BUT SO IS PIVOTING

Whether in sales, leadership, or chasing personal goals, persistence is an extremely valuable trait. But learning the art of the pivot can be just as valuable.

Two things can help you know when to pivot.

One is to have wide enough knowledge of options available to you. In the example I just shared, carefully observing the full range of office needs of the business I was selling to, coupled with what I knew about the IBM dictation system, allowed me to confidently and seamlessly change what I was selling.

The other helpful skill in pivoting is to know when further persistence is not going to pay off. If you stop because it is getting too hard, that's a problem. If it's because you have objectively sized up the situation and see your current plan is not working, that's the perfect time for a pivot.

After five years, I was happy with my successes, but I became bored selling the same office products. So I decided to get a real estate license.

When I told my boss my plans, he encouraged me to take a beat.

"Do yourself a favor and interview with the computing division," he said. That division was selling a computer-based word processor. Although it was a great piece of technology, IBM was still struggling to sell it. The division's sales team knew the ins and outs of the technology itself, but they didn't know the office environment or fully understand the needs of potential users.

My knowledge of the inner workings of the office environment won me a transfer to the company's General Systems Division. The real estate plan was shelved, and I dove into my new role. I did need training on this new complicated technology, but once I understood it, I got excited. It married what an office system should do with state of the art computing power (at that time anyway!) Once I saw its value for business, I was confident that it would be "a piece of cake" to sell.

Here is what I did not factor into my excitement: Because this system was expensive, it would require a much longer sales process than I was used to. It also always involved going out to bid against other companies. That meant I would be directly competing with one or two other salespeople and systems for every sale I was trying to make.

Before becoming the specialist in the Portland office for this newer technology, I was used to selling products ranging from electronic typewriters, dictation equipment and copiers, on a much faster and more frequent basis. This was different, and adjusting to the longer sales cycle was frustrating.

Before long, I looked up and I was three or four months into the new job and I still didn't have a single sale. When you are used to weekly successes, that's a loooong drought. After failing to win any of the bids I submitted, my frustration was getting close to despair.

Around this time, my branch manager Tom Jenkins was walking by my desk. He paused for a moment and said to me, "It's always darkest before the dawn."

That was it. His words were simple, direct, and exactly what I needed to hear.

In that moment I knew Tom was paying attention and understood my situation. He could see I was working hard. He knew I was coming from a division where success came much more regularly. And he could sense my frustration.

He saw there was no need for a lengthy pep talk. He also wasn't the kind of leader who thought that additional pressure or subtle threats about performance are the right tools. He knew this was not the time to be sending the message, "What have you done for me lately?"

Tom understood I needed to hear a simple and direct message, which is what he delivered. No more, no less. He also turned out to be a bit of a prophet, because less than a week later the dark evaporated and the dawn finally broke.

The beeper on my page went off, indicating I had an incoming phone call. It turned out to be the purchasing department calling to tell me I had won and they had accepted my bid. Because I had become so used to hearing the opposite, my immediate reaction was to say, "Really? You're not calling to tell me that I *didn't* get it?" We laughed and I was on my way to better times and more sales.

LESSON #4: THE POWER OF THE RIGHT WORDS AT THE RIGHT TIME

At the time Tom said those words to me, I wasn't aware he was paying close attention to how I was doing or how hard I was working. That one sentence, "It's always darkest before the dawn," told me he saw exactly what was going on.

A good leader knows what his team members are dealing with and how they are approaching their work, especially challenges they are confronting.

Is the person struggling with something new? Have they been putting in the work consistently and persistently? Every situation can be different, but putting some thought into figuring out the right words and delivering them at the right time can have an outsized impact.

You will be recognized as a true leader when you learn the ability to be there for your people when they need it the most. What Tom revealed to me in that moment was, "I see you and what you have been doing, and I appreciate it, and it will work out." It is these kinds of moments that generate true respect, loyalty and credibility toward you as a leader.

VIRTUAL WORK ENVIRONMENTS

It is worth noting here the workplace has evolved considerably. Especially in the days since the COVID epidemic, virtual and remote work have become more common. While some have pushed back against this trend, many businesses have embraced it wholeheartedly.

If you find yourself as a leader in a virtual environment, whether you love it or hate it or are somewhere in between, you need to recognize that it is important to make a special effort to observe what people are doing every day even when you can't see them.

Because we were in the office together every day, Tom could see that I was coming to work early. He could observe how I was handling bids. He could pick up on my mental outlook.

In a virtual environment, that day-to-day in-person interaction doesn't happen. The small talk that takes place at the coffee machine may no longer be available. If so, don't complain about it or play the victim. Find other ways to connect with the individuals on your team and make an extra effort to know exactly what is going on with them. And always look for opportunities to catch them doing something right instead of looking for what they're doing wrong. (We will pick up this theme in more detail in a later chapter about delivering quality feedback.)

CHAPTER 3

LEARN TO QUIT TALKING BEFORE THE OTHER PERSON STOPS LISTENING

Tom Jenkins taught me another valuable lesson, and again it came in the form of a short, direct phrase.

One day in the office, he asked about the status of a particular bid. I launched into a long monologue, giving him the history of what I had done, what I planned to do next, details of the prospective client, and more. On and on I went.

When I finally stopped, Tom said, "Elaine, you need to learn to quit talking before I stop listening."

It was as if Tom only wanted to know what time it was, but I had decided to build a clock in front of him.

Tom was communicating two things to me. One: speak in headlines whenever possible (more on this in a moment).

Two: he was giving me a clue to one of the most overlooked but also most important skills a leader needs: sensory acuity. That may sound like a fancy technical term, but at its heart, it means making accurate observations about the impact you are having on others.

Recall from the book's introduction one of Ross Perot's specific criticisms of my presentation at the bank. He was upset that the room was too dark during the PowerPoint presentation so there was no way to know how the audience was receiving it.

Perot was really pointing out a violation of the principle of sensory acuity. You cannot accurately assess people's reactions when you can't see them.

Had I been paying attention to Tom as I droned on about that particular bid, I could have stopped my monologue and simply given him a succinct status of the bid. Tom made me aware that I should have been asking myself: "Are you paying attention to my reaction to what you are telling me?"

In that example, I was talking to my boss. But sensory acuity is even more important from the leadership side of the equation. Too many leaders think that "everyone will (or should) listen to me just by virtue of the fact that I am the boss."

The best leaders know better. Relying solely on your authority as the boss will have diminishing returns, as your team will come to expect bloated and boring messages from you. As a leader, you should not monopolize your team's time just because you think you can.

Pausing for engagement is also another effective tactic. Stop your monologue and ask questions. Slow down for a minute and give the other person a chance to speak. Someone told me once that the art of being a good listener is to be easy to interrupt. The more reactions you are aware of, the more sensory acuity data you will have to help you.

Great leaders become artful communicators by learning to pay attention to their "audiences" reactions (even if that audience is one person, as will often be the case). What's their body language tell you? What sounds or gestures are they making? What can you tell from their facial expressions? Train yourself to see all these things.

Your interpretations may not be right every single time, but the more you focus on and practice sensory acuity, the better you will get at it. And the better you get at it, the easier it will be to adapt in real time to the needs of your audience.

LESSON #5: PAY ATTENTION TO NON-VERBAL CUES WHEN COMMUNICATING

Any time you are communicating, whether on stage, in a meeting, or one-on-one, pay close attention to body language and facial expressions. This is crucial feedback on how well you are communicating your message.

Learn to adjust on the fly, and pause frequently to engage the other person(s) to get a sense of their level of reception and understanding of what you are saying.

Related: See Chapter 13: The Power of Questions for more on how to best engage and communicate.

There is a second key point inside the message of "learn to stop talking before I stop listening." That is the skill of speaking in headlines.

Think of it this way: For decades, each major broadcast network has had a nightly show summing up the news of world news in 30 minutes. I can't think of a better example of how to sort through vast amounts of information and then communicate what is most important as concisely as possible.

Whether they do it perfectly every time is not the point. Rather, if a team can present a coherent picture of the news of the world in just 30 minutes, surely you can boil down your own messages so you are only sharing what the other person needs to know.

No matter how important the message, there is almost always a way to synthesize the key points to make it more concise. Returning to the nightly news example, they are able to cut down a report on, say, a complex piece of legislation to two minutes and still give their viewers a grasp of what it is and why it matters. But somehow you cannot streamline your ten minute meeting presentation to your team down to five minutes? Of course you can.

What this takes is exercising your brain and asking what is the most important point. Once you know that, ask yourself what is absolutely essential to communicating it. Finally, challenge yourself to get it down to a size that fits an appropriate time frame.

This is especially crucial when presenting to those above you in the hierarchy of the organization. Whenever I had an upcoming presentation of 30 minutes, I would still spend up to five hours preparing just for the presentation. And these presentations would be on a topic I already knew quite well!

It was not enough just to "know my stuff." I had to figure out what was most crucial, and boil it down and communicate it so that busy executives could understand and ultimately be persuaded to take whatever action I was advocating.

This takes time, effort and intention. A presentation is not so much about preparing slides (although that matters, too), but about applying critical thinking to decide what really needs to be said to this particular audience.

Remember, too, this ability does not just apply to presentations, but also in everyday communication with those around you. Find ways to be more crisp, clear and concise in how you speak and persuade.

You do not need to worry that speaking in headlines will leave out important things. When your audience needs to know more, they'll ask. Leaving room for questions will reveal to you what matters to them, and that is also valuable information.

I can't emphasize enough that focused, concise communication takes more time to craft, not less. There is a quote sometimes attributed to Mark Twain that is appropriate: "I didn't have time to write a short letter, so I wrote a long one instead."

We will continue with this theme in the next chapter, where I talk about how I learned to take this skill to an even deeper level.

LESSON #6: SPEAK IN HEADLINES

Always look for ways to cut down your messages to the most important and essential information. This applies to all situations:

- Everyday commonplace scenarios where you are asked for an update, teaching a skill, etc.

- In meetings, when it is your time to give input, whether as a contributor or leader.

- In big presentations to your own team, or in presenting to a team that you need to persuade (client or executives or both).

Also remember that as a leader, you should not assume that you are owed a long attention span from your team just because you are in charge. You'll ultimately earn that right by being respectful of their time and by working hard to cut down your messages to what matters.

One very good practical rule of thumb. If you are planning on communicating for a certain amount of time, ask yourself how to cut it to half as long. Your message will almost always have a greater impact and be the better for it.

CHAPTER 4

CUT DOWN YOUR COMMUNICATION TO THE LENGTH OF A RIDE TO THE AIRPORT

During my time with IBM, I was always impressed with the culture, and one of its particular strengths was developing leaders. IBM did more than talk about leadership development; they offered concrete programs to allow people to progress to greater levels of responsibility.

Among their techniques was "special assignments." These were opportunities to see what the company looked like at the top levels. How did the senior executives operate? How did the team around them provide support?

That is how I found myself working in the IBM president's office one summer. Mostly this meant assisting the staff who supported him, but there were precious opportunities spent with the president that gave me a window on what his business life was like.

I remember one amusing situation where the president was ready to do a live national address to all employees. Nearing the time for him to speak, I noticed something that prompted me to grab a hair dryer. I stood patiently by him with the dryer in my hand as he continued to prepare. Eventually he looked up.

"What are you doing with that hair dryer?" He did not have a lot of hair, so he was even more perplexed by what I might be doing.

"That apple you ate got some juice on your tie," I said.

He looked down and smiled. He handed me his tie, I dried it, and he put it back on and gave his speech. This is an admittedly very small example of a key principle that we will develop more later in this chapter and throughout this book: anticipation. In this case, it was to know what the leader needs and figure out how you can support them

The more you learn about anticipating, the more you learn to think like a leader. The results can be amazing.

It became clear to me early on that there were two things to be figured out when working with a top-flight executive: how can you carve out pockets of time with someone who has so many priorities? And once you have that slice of time, how do you make the most of it?

Here is how we solved the "pockets of time" issue with the IBM president. His role of course involved a fair amount of flying, and the drive from the office to the airport was typically around 30 minutes or so. This was a time before cell phones, so this was a golden opportunity to have his attention.

Next, we needed to use it to maximum effect.

We would hop in the limo with him on the way to the airport with several issues prepared for him to review. He would read the synopsis of the issue we provided. We would include three or four options for addressing it, and list the pros and cons of each. As a team, we also gave our recommendation of what we believed to be the best choice.

We kept going from one issue to the next until we arrived at the airport. I started to keep track of how often the president agreed with our recommended solution. I also tracked when his decision went in a completely different direction or he chose one of the other options.

This experience was superb. For one, I got very good at speaking in headlines. This was communication synthesis on steroids. The time to the airport was all we had available to us – it was our "world news" television slot. We had to determine what the top stories were, provide a concise synopsis and objective analysis, and guard against including extraneous information.

Tracking his responses also proved to be very beneficial. When he took our recommendation, that was a type of feedback. It told us that we were on the right track and thinking in a way that was adding value to the company.

When he went in a different direction, that was an even bigger learning opportunity. The question then became: What did he see that we did not? What factors led to his decision? What mental filters did he use to make decisions?

The answers were valuable for two reasons. One, the more we could see how he thought – especially what he considered as relevant – the better we'd be able to analyze future issues. Learn, get better, repeat.

The other value is how it taught us to think like a leader, especially one at the highest echelon of a profession. Wherever I have been around senior leadership, I consider it a unique opportunity to observe that quality as closely as possible. My precise purpose was to learn how to analyze and think like the best.

You do not need to be assigned to an executive or work in close proximity to one to put this into practice. (Although if you do get those opportunities, be a sponge!). I remember my very first staff assignment with IBM was in their Denver office. The Regional Manager's technique of communication was to have his team write up a summary of whatever issues they were working on. He would then take that raw information and turn it into a polished memo to the whole office so everyone would stay on top of things.

I began studying what he did. I looked at the mechanics of how he took raw information and transformed it into a solid piece of communication. What did he leave out? What did he leave in? What mattered and why? All this studying and observing enabled me to eventually write those memos for him in his voice.

LESSON #7: OBSERVE GREATNESS AND GO AND DO LIKEWISE

Anytime you get a chance to observe leaders (good or bad or somewhere in between), you have an opportunity. Naturally, a great model is best of all, because mostly what you learn from a poor leader is what not to do.

Do not think that if you haven't been assigned to work with a top executive that you cannot use this technique. You should be on the alert every day for ways to learn from more seasoned leaders.

One especially good tip is to notice when they do something unexpected, or something that makes you scratch your head. That is where learning goes into turbocharge mode, because it is not something you could come up with at your current level of knowledge. Pick apart why and how they may have come up with the decision or direction that they did. What does it show you?

Related: See the next lesson below in this chapter. It is important not just to "take" from the leader. Do more than just learn; add value. There is an adage that you will likely be doing your next job for six months before you are actually promoted to that job. The key is to always look for ways to add value beyond your current role.

Something else to keep in mind is that always looking to the boss to provide every answer is a broken leadership model. Yes, you want to learn from the top leaders and be guided by them when appropriate. But you'll never be a true leader if you always play it safe as a follower and expect answers to be handed to you.

By putting yourself inside the mind of the leader you will be on the right track. To get respect and earn promotions, you have to show what you can offer to the business by bringing your own ideas and demonstrating the value you have to offer.

Do this by acting "as if":

- Act as *if* you already have the position you want. Get in the habit of thinking like someone who carefully considers the implications of new ideas and initiatives, someone who can see with a wide-ranging lens.

- Act as *if* you can put yourself in your bosses' shoes. This is not the same as looking to a leader for all the answers. It is looking to see how a leader comes up with answers, and using the same pattern to get better at finding solutions yourself.

LESSON #8: ACT "AS IF"

Once you are in a position of leadership (or when you want to get promoted to your first leadership job), do not wait for people to tell you what and how to do everything.

It is a common mistake to believe that if you just do a good enough job in your current role, that should be enough to earn you a new role with more responsibility. No! You need to think and act like you have already reached the next step up the ladder.

Your goal should be to observe how leaders think and act, and then show them how you can add value, not just be a drain on their time.

CHAPTER 5

ARE YOU THE AVON LADY?

A few chapters ago I mentioned that being one of the first women to sell for IBM sometimes got me in the door, if for no other reason than the novelty. The business owner wanted to see what this was all about.

But of course, it was not always positive. I remember people making just about any other assumption than that I was there to sell technology products. Once while sitting in a prospect's office waiting to see the owner I was asked, "Are you the Avon lady?"

Drawing on as much patience as I could muster, I said, "No, I am your IBM sales rep." Beyond being mistaken for the Avon lady, there were other hazards to being a woman in the world of business.

One Valentine's Day in 1988 was particularly memorable. I was in an airport in Lubbock, Texas, waiting for a flight back to Denver (my home base at the time). Up strode a man decked out like a dandy cowboy, complete with boots and a ten-gallon hat.

"What's a pretty little heifer like you doing in an airport on Valentine's Day?" he asked.

If that was his idea of a good opening line, let's just say it failed spectacularly. Later on the phone with my boss at IBM I remember saying, "I've got to get out of here and back to Denver!"

Another memorable incident also involved flying. This was later in my career when I was working for British Telecom. There were offices in both London and Atlanta, and five of us were flying from one to the other via British Airways. For whatever reason, there were only four first-class tickets so the airline assigned me a seat in coach.

When I asked the British Airways clerk why, I was told because I was the only woman, they assumed I was the lowest-ranking team member. The truth was the opposite; I was the highest rank of the group. When I got back to Atlanta, I mentioned this incident to my boss, and he filed a complaint with British Airways.

At least I got some satisfaction out of this incident. Not only did I get a free upgrade to first class the next time I flew, but the British Airways staff and attendants fawned over me to the point that the person sitting next to me asked if I was someone famous.

While these stories have a funny side, they also have a darker side to them. In some ways, it could be easy to get bitter and frustrated when you are treated negatively based on false assumptions or backward beliefs.

Of course, it is also just plain wrong, and nothing I am going to say in the rest of this chapter is meant to say that people being treated differently based on their personal characteristics is acceptable.

What I will advocate for is to refuse any kind of victim thinking.

This is the perfect place to introduce my #1 book recommendation for leaders. I'll be sharing many titles that I am passionate about, but if you could only read one, make it *The Art of Possibility: Transforming Professional and Personal Life* by Rosamund Stone Zander and Benjamin Zander.

BOOK RECOMMENDATION:
THE ART OF POSSIBILITY

Written by Rosamund Stone Zander, a family therapist and executive coach, and Benjamin Zander, a world-renowned conductor, this book encourages you to become the framework for everything that happens in your life. I cannot recommend it highly enough.

Bonus tip: The audio version is fantastic. Because of Benjamin Zander's musical background and talent, music is beautifully integrated with the inspiring stories and ideas in the book. Listening to it is a transformational experience.

The entire book is worth reading, but I want to focus on Chapter 10, "Being the Board."

Using the metaphor of chess, the chapter challenges the reader to make a choice. Do you want to be a chess piece in life, a pawn left to fate and the actions of others? Or do you want to be the chess board itself, and take full responsibility for how your life plays out?

The Zanders encourage you to affirm that "I am the framework for everything that happens in my life."

The example they use might sound radical at first, but it is worth reflecting on to see the deeper point. They say to imagine you are sitting in your car, stopped at a red traffic light. Suddenly a drunk driver slams into you from behind. Who is at fault?

As the Zanders point out, according to the law, it's a no-brainer. Morally and legally, the drunk driver is at fault. The driver will need to suffer the consequences of his or her actions.

However, if you want to live as someone "being the board," you take a different perspective. What is your role in what happened? If you are honest, every time you get in the car, you accept a certain amount of risk. Yes, most of the time you can count on the other drivers to be reasonable enough to not slam into you out of nowhere. But you also know it's not 100 percent certain that won't ever happen. Every time you step in the car, you acknowledge that statistically you are taking a risk.

For any situation, always start by asking, "What was my role in this?" That will allow you to gain insights you would otherwise miss when you are looking to blame someone or something else. In this case, the faulty assumption was: "I will never have a car wreck if I drive safely."

Taking this level of responsibility for your life is challenging if you are only using moral and legal perspectives. It is tempting (and easier) to slide toward a victim mentality. This is especially true when from a strictly moral and legal perspective, you are right.

But a big part of "Being the Board" is escaping the "You're wrong, I'm right" paradigm. Once you decide that you are the framework for everything that happens in your life, it is extremely empowering.

For any situation or circumstance, ask "What was my role and what can I learn from it?" When you ask that, your power is restored. This is very similar to a favorite saying of Tony Robbins: "Everything happens for *you* and not *to* you."

LESSON #9: YOU ARE THE FRAMEWORK FOR EVERYTHING THAT HAPPENS IN YOUR LIFE

The first and primary skill of a leader is to take radical responsibility for everything that happens. Even negative events offer chances to learn. Keep in mind that everything is happening for you and not to you.

Also remember that as a leader, modeling this for your team is crucial. You are setting the tone for how your team will respond to adversity. How you respond will be contagious. If you invest time complaining about the decisions made outside of your control, or market conditions, or how unfairly you have been treated, that is what you can expect to be mirrored back to you from your team.

If you step up and decide to be the framework for everything in your life, you will become a respected and empowered leader.

One of my favorite quotes from the *Art of Possibility* underscores why you want to do this: "The purpose of naming yourself as the board, or as the context in which life occurs to you, is to give yourself the power to transform your experience of any unwanted condition into one with which you care to live."

Related: See Lesson #24: Find a Way to Free Yourself from Negative Dynamics with Others. We are often quick to judge others for certain behaviors, and then eventually discover we sometimes act the exact same way!

At the outset of this chapter, I described how outside forces made decisions about my status because I am a woman. That put a fork in the road for me.

One path was to focus on that negativity and things I could not control. I could have taken the way of finding and assigning blame. A clue that we are headed in the wrong direction is to use the word "because" to explain things.

If we say, "This happened BECAUSE [insert something you cannot control]," we are no longer being the board. Statements like this are non-starters:

- I do not have a chance at this *because* I have an art history degree and not a finance degree.

- I will lose out to another candidate *because* they went to Harvard and I didn't.

- I cannot get promoted *because* I'm too old (or I'm too young, I don't have the right background, etc.)

- I won't be able to reach a senior leadership position *because* there is a glass ceiling for women. (I recall having vigorous debates with my coach at one point in my career. I insisted there WAS a glass ceiling and she helped me see that the glass ceiling only existed because I believed it was there).

Once you go down the "road of because," you'll always end up on a dead-end street. Shutting things down with a definitive "because" closes you off to what you can control and to what can be opportunities or ways to change the game.

What are some better uses of language to frame an analysis of a setback? Instead of using "because" statements, try asking open-ended questions:

- What didn't I see?

- What else could I have done?

- What was my role in this?

- How can I move beyond a simple binary right-wrong analysis and see this in a wider perspective?

NAVIGATING OUR OWN BIASES

Good leaders look for ways to eliminate bias because it skews reality. Great leaders know that the right question to ask is not "Am I biased?" The answer to that is obviously yes, because we all have a certain lens rooted in our individual experiences.

The right question is, "What are my biases?" And the right follow-up is, "What is the best way to correct for my biases?"

A good place to start is to ask "What other perspectives could be useful here? And how do I get those perspectives?"

Notice how this shifts the whole notion of how to overcome biases to a positive footing. Instead of using shutdown, binary, yes-no questions, the good leader uses open-ended questions and goes on a search for other perspectives.

Respected leaders use a framework rooted in openness instead of a blame-hunting mentality. They combine that with a commitment to always avoid a victim mentality.

CHAPTER 6

WITTGENSTEIN MADE PRACTICAL

I eventually became head of sales training for IBM at the company's education center in Atlanta. This opened up a particularly exciting opportunity for me.

IBM's Director of Strategy had connected with the amazingly interesting philosopher Fernando Flores. What a background Fernando has! Engineer. Philosopher. Entrepreneur. Politician. Political prisoner. And eventually researcher at Stanford University.

Born in Chile, he became the country's finance minister in 1972 for the government headed then by Salvatore Allende. After Allende was overthrown in a coup led by Augusto Pinochet in 1973, Flores went from high-ranking government official to political prisoner for three years. Finally through the efforts of Amnesty International, he was released from prison and exiled to the United States, and that's how he ended up at Stanford.

While at Stanford, Flores made a deal with IBM. The company would send him a small group of people one week a month for five months. He said under his guidance, he could transform those people into "observers." What he meant by observers were individuals he would train to see the world in a different way. This ability would give them greater clarity and open them up to see possibilities that others could not.

The Director of Strategy sent word that he wanted someone nominated from the training center to be one of the participants. It was my great fortune to be selected. So once a month I flew to California and spent a week taking part in Flores' training program.

This was the 1980s when a business philosophy known as Total Quality Management (TQM) was all the rage. This strategy had proven extremely successful for businesses in Japan. Flores believed TQM worked very well for machine environments and assembly lines, because those are very linear processes. But something more nuanced and complex was required for how humans work together. Flores understood that people work things out through conversation, which is not a linear process.

He had studied the German philosopher Ludwig Wittgenstein to come up with his own method and philosophy. Wittgenstein's writing was known for being particularly abstract and difficult, but Flores was able to translate his ideas about "speech acts" into a practical system for how communication drives action in a business.

Here it is in a nutshell.

First, he recognized that one of the most fundamental aspects of business is coordinating the actions of a team. You really cannot accomplish anything without coordinating action unless one person literally does everything.

Next he looked at interpersonal processes people used to coordinate actions together. How is it actually done?

Using his observations with some help from Wittgenstein's concepts, he realized it is a four-step process, which he broke down into quadrants.

Basic Action Workflow

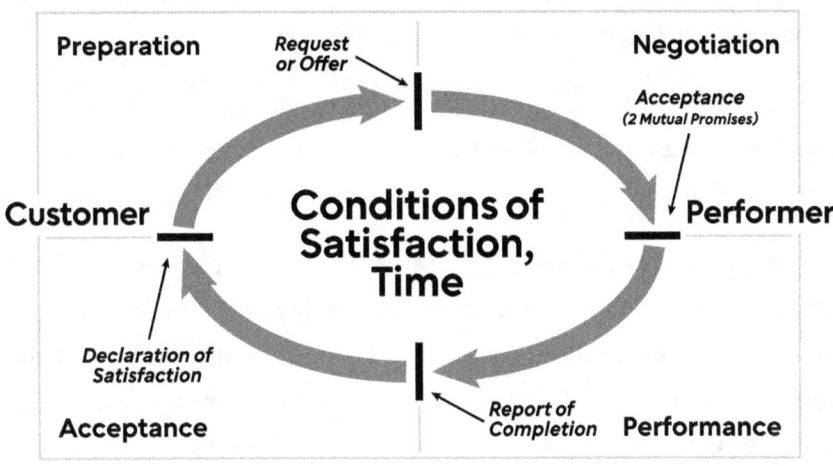

Created by Fernando Flores

The first quadrant of Basic Action Workflow starts with Preparation. This is where someone requests an action from someone else. For simplicity, let's say it could be a manager telling an employee that she wants a report delivered by Monday.

The second quadrant is Negotiation. This could be as simple as the employee agreeing that he could accomplish the report by Monday. Or perhaps he works with his boss to be able to have a couple of extra days and deliver it on Wednesday. Whatever the case, the key is that through negotiation there is clear agreement on what needs to be done and by when.

Next comes the third quadrant, Performance. This simply means completing what was agreed upon. In our example, the employee does the report and submits it on time.

The fourth and final quadrant closes the loop of the process and is called Acceptance. In our example, after receiving and reviewing the report, the manager acknowledges completion.

It is in this last quadrant where there is so much opportunity for leaders, and these possibilities are often wasted. I'll get to that in a minute, but first I want to pause here for a moment to emphasize something important.

I strongly recommend reviewing these four quadrants again, and then reflecting on them. They are kind of deceptively simple at first glance. But once you start using these quadrants to think through your own team's workflow process, it will help you see with greater clarity how you coordinate action. It will also help you diagnose where breakdowns occur so you can stop them from happening in the future.

Be prepared: once you begin using this framework, you will begin to see the Preparation-Negotiation-Performance-Acceptance quadrant flow everywhere. It becomes a pair of glasses to look out at the world, and every time something goes wrong, you will look to the loop to figure out where. It really gets at something fundamental.

If all this talk of quadrants and loops seems too theoretical at first, start applying it to practical situations.. Here is an example:

SCENARIO: LAUNCHING A MARKETING CAMPAIGN

1. PREPARATION

The Marketing Director tells the Social Media Manager:

"I need a campaign plan for our new product launch, and I want it ready by next Friday."

This is the request for action — initiating the workflow.

2. NEGOTIATION

The Social Media Manager replies:

"Next Friday is doable, but I'll need the product specs by Tuesday and access to the design assets by Wednesday."

The Director agrees and commits to providing those inputs on time.

Here, both parties align on expectations, resources, and deadlines. A mutual commitment is formed.

3. PERFORMANCE

The Social Media Manager:

- Gets the specs on Tuesday
- Uses the design assets from Wednesday
- Creates and refines the campaign plan
- Submits the completed plan to the Director on Thursday

This is the doing — the agreed action being carried out.

4. ACCEPTANCE

The Director reviews the plan:

"This is exactly what we needed and here's why." The director offers specifics. (More on the concept of specific feedback below). Acceptance is an acknowledgment of completion, and if it is done right, it closes the action loop.

Note that this is also a powerful framework for figuring out where something went wrong. For example, what if during the negotiation step, the social media manager had NOT said she would need the specs by Tuesday?

This could have led to a breakdown. She might not have received the specs until Thursday afternoon and the deadline would have been missed.

If you filter all breakdowns through these four quadrants, you will learn to pinpoint more specifically where things went wrong and then know how to fix it in the future.

LESSON #10: ANALYZE WORKFLOW TO FIND BREAKDOWNS AND FIX THEM

Everything you do as a leader involves coordinating action. The quadrants of Preparation-Negotiation-Performance-Acceptance gives you a simple but powerful framework for analyzing how well that coordination is happening.

Use this tool consistently, especially when you need to figure out the reason for breakdowns. Soon it will become almost second nature to see the workflow through this lens. Of course, it is crucial to not just analyze, but then use it to fix what is wrong. Those corrections will be much easier because you have taken the time to pinpoint where the disconnect happened.

Related: See Chapter 12, The Billion Dollar Lesson, for more on how to analyze when something goes wrong.

Now let's return to the topic of the fourth quadrant, Acceptance. There are a lot of unrealized opportunities packed within this area. (In fact, these opportunities are the topic of my first book, *Making Feedback Work*).

Acceptance can look like this:

- "Thank you for completing the report." And then nothing else. The report is accepted and no more is said about it.

Acceptance can also look like this:

- "Thank you for completing the report. Good job. I really appreciate you and all that you do, your work is fantastic."

Which is better?

Trick question. The answer is neither. They are both missed opportunities. The first one only acknowledges that the work was completed. The second one does that, too, but also adds what seems like good, positive feedback.

The truth is that the second one may even be a little worse because it creates the illusion that real feedback has happened, when in fact all that was handed out were happy platitudes.

And this is how many, many people in leadership positions think of feedback. They think of it as some version of "good job." Or on the flip side. communicating that, "I'm vaguely displeased or disappointed." Neither works.

The Acceptance quadrant should be used to deliver specific and fact-based assertions, not hazy compliments or unclear criticism.

I call platitudes and vague, happy compliments "empty calorie" feedback. It tastes good, but in a half hour you are hungry again. It's not that there is something wrong with being positive. In fact, managers of all types usually need to make more of a point of calling out what's right. The issue is you just need to make that positive feedback more substantial and filling by being specific.

The key is to *identify specific behaviors* and call those out for their good or bad impact. This gives your team something to work with when adjusting their actions and output (or in keeping up what they are already doing).

To do it right, use a three-step model when delivering feedback:

- Identify the specific behavior.
- Describe the impact of that behavior.
- Discuss the future desired behaviors.

Another key for great feedback is to dive deeply into this question: how am I measuring good?

Surprisingly, a lot of people in leadership positions cannot answer this question with much clarity. You need to formulate a specific set of criteria that is quantifiable: Behaviors you can see and metrics you can objectively measure.

This will take biases and favoritism out of how people are managed, which will also charge up your culture in an extremely productive way. When you manage with clear assertions grounded in fact, it is energizing. People are attracted to a strong culture where it is crystal clear what is considered good performance.

AN EXCERPT FROM MY FIRST BOOK,
MAKING FEEDBACK WORK:

An Effective Feedback Model Has Three Parts

The three parts are:

  Part One: Identify the specific behavior

  Part Two: Describe the impact

  Part Three: Discuss the future desired behavior

Here are a few simple examples to demonstrate how both positive and constructive feedback includes all three parts:

Positive Feedback

I noticed you submitted the report early, thank you! (Specific Behavior)

Now I'll be able to move forward with the project earlier than planned. (Impact)

I appreciate your initiative and hope you'll continue to support the team in this way. (Future behavior)

Constructive Feedback

I noticed you were ten minutes late to the last two meetings. (Specific Behavior)

We had to start the meeting later than planned which inconvenienced the rest of the team. (Impact)

Please be on time going forward. (Future behavior)

BOOK RECOMMENDATION: *CONVERSATIONS FOR ACTION AND COLLECTED ESSAYS*

If you want to dive even deeper on the topics of Basic Action Workflow and Speech Acts, I highly recommend the book Conversations for Action and Collected Essays by Fernando Flores (edited by Maria Flores Letelier).

It is not possible to do justice to Flores' ideas in a few paragraphs. It is worth your time to get the book. In particular, the book's first five chapters lay out the foundations for a deeper understanding of these concepts.

As you become more familiar with his ideas on workflow, you will see that any "breakdown" in a business can generally be traced back to failing to complete one of the four quadrants. It is a great diagnostic tool for determining when something doesn't go according to plan. It also prevents discussions from digressing into the "blame game".

The lessons I am sharing here are also anchored in what I learned from Flores. He talked about Wittgenstein's different kinds of "speech acts." One of those acts is an Assessment, which is an opinion formed from feelings and snap judgments. This should be avoided when giving feedback.

Another kind of speech act is an Assertion. In this act, you make assertions based on fact. Great feedback is rooted in this kind of speech act.

Much of a company's culture hinges on the fourth quadrant. When their actions are completed, do your team members know where they stand? Are they getting specific feedback based on clear standards? Or are they getting "feel good" or vague feedback that essentially communicates nothing? It makes all the difference.

LESSON #11: MAKE FEEDBACK SPECIFIC AND OBJECTIVE

Start by establishing the criteria to answer this question: How am I measuring what is considered "good"? This needs to be fact-based and something that can be observed and measured.

Next, when you provide feedback, always do three things:

- Identify a specific behavior
- Describe the impact of that action
- Discuss the future desired behavior (either more of the same, or a corrected path forward).

Put all this in the context of the quadrants explained earlier in the chapter. The fourth quadrant is a wonderful opportunity to reinforce good actions and eliminate bad actions in the future. Do not waste it.

One final thought: make a conscious effort to call out the good. Too many times we fall into the trap of only providing feedback when something goes wrong.

CHAPTER 7

HOW DO I GET PROMOTED?

In Chapter 4 we explored one of the key principles for making yourself promotable: Act "as if." That is a huge part of it, but what more should you be doing?

When you are in a leadership position, one of the most frequent questions you will hear is: "How do I get promoted?"

A good place to start is David Maester's book *The Trusted Advisor*. One of the companies where I worked used this as a guide for building trust-based, long-term client relationships.

Trust-based skills work also for internal corporate relationships. To get promoted, a person should work hard at building trust within the organization. But what does that look like?

As explained in the book, trustworthiness is credibility + reliability + intimacy, divided by self-orientation. (This "Trust Equation" was developed by Charles Green, David Maister, and Robert Galford).

Credibility and reliability come from doing what you say and being accountable for your actions. Intimacy in this case obviously does not refer to the romantic usage. It is more about a willingness to be open, honest, and vulnerable.

But what does "divided by" self-orientation mean? This is simply an acknowledgment that careers and client relationships can be derailed by self-orientation or always thinking in terms of "what's in it for me?"

You can be completely credible, super reliable, and be open to having difficult conversations. But all of those positives can dissolve if your colleagues and clients sense that your primary goal is promoting your own agenda.

So to sum it up simply, if you want to get promoted, do this:

- Build trust by being accountable, reliable, and honest.
- Do not undermine that trust with a relentless "me-first" attitude.

Another helpful framework to make yourself promotable is to think of leadership as if you are an orchestra conductor. I first learned of this from the work of Roger Nierenberg, founder of the Music Paradigm and author of *Maestro: A Surprising Story About Leading by Listening*.

Nierenberg notes that conducting is very much like what great leaders do in business. Standing on the podium, the conductor is the only one who can see everything. No one stands behind conductors telling them what to do. Conductors see the whole, and with that vantage point comes the expectation that they take responsibility for everything in front of them.

When it comes to moving up in your career, this is an important mindset to adopt. Let's walk through how this process often unfolds.

You get your first promotion to a leadership position. It is exciting, you know it is going to be great, especially having more power... and then reality hits. You still have people to whom you are reporting and they expect you to help them look good and accomplish their goals. But you also now have people reporting to you, and you will be judged on their performance.

Before, when you were only a sole contributor, you had complete control of your performance. Now you will be judged on how well you can coordinate others on whom you will be relying.

On top of that, you will have to put out fires, handle the complaints of your direct reports, all while implementing initiatives coming from higher up in the organization.

The first couple of rungs up the ladder can be a daunting adjustment. Here are two things that will help.

First, set up a consistent structure for communicating with your boss. If you want help and support, your own manager needs to know what you are accomplishing and at least the broad outlines of how you are doing it. It is all about managing your manager's expectations. Or saying it another way, there should be "no surprises".

You might be thinking, "Of course my boss knows what I am doing!" You may be surprised to learn that's often not the case. They have a lot on their own full plates. They are dealing with their own pressures, and are looking out from their own podiums at an even bigger orchestra. Their focus will not be entirely on you and your work.

That's why it is key to routinely update them in writing. You can negotiate how often to send those updates (weekly, monthly, etc.). You could email them every Monday morning or the start of the month with the following:

- What I/my team accomplished the previous week/month. Be sure to include both achievements and setbacks.

- What I/my team plans to accomplish this week/month.

- What support you need to meet your goals for this week/month or the near future.

Some bosses will instantly love this proactive approach, while others will say I don't need this information. If your boss is in the latter camp, explain that you are doing it in part to discipline yourself as a leader who stays on top of things. And it's true: the value of doing this consistently will benefit you even more than your boss.

What you will discover is that those above you will not only appreciate what you are doing, but see you as a person ready to be promoted sooner rather than later.

It is important to emphasize that you should keep up this communication with unwavering consistency. Many people start this practice, but after a few weeks or months, let it slide. When you stick with it, you create a documented trail to show if there's ever a question about what you've been doing and communicating to your boss. And your boss will also appreciate your professionalism.

LESSON #12: CONSISTENT, WRITTEN COMMUNICATION IS A WINNING DISCIPLINE

To earn increasing responsibility and promotions, one of your best friends should be regular written communication.

The main purpose of the communication should cover three main points:

- What you have accomplished
- What you will do next
- What support you will need to accomplish it

There is no reason to go overboard with the length of your update. Just speak in headlines and if someone needs more information, they'll ask. In most cases, they will appreciate the clear, concise information.

If you do not do this, it is likely that the people you report to will have only a vague sense of what you are doing.

Mandel Communications (www.mandel.com) is another resource for tips on becoming an expert communicator, especially their method known as SCIPAB (Situation, Complication, Position, Action, Benefit). Effective communication is filtered through all six of these categories.

Here's a greatly simplified example using SCIPAB:

- **Situation:** We promised the client a deliverable by June 1st.

- **Complication:** We do not have the resources to meet that deadline.

- **Implications:** We could lose this client and damage our reputation in the industry.

- **Position:** We need to negotiate a new due date.

- **Action:** I will call the client tomorrow to work out a new due date.

- **Benefit:** The client's business and trust are retained.

SCIPAB is an effective tool for reducing communication to the essentials.

GET MORE PEOPLE IN YOUR CANOE TO HELP YOU PADDLE

Another key skill for young leaders is to find ways to be less isolated. New leaders often get frustrated when they feel they cannot get an organization to move forward with positive initiatives. Regular, consistent written communication can help you build connections with the people you report to, but there are other ways to build bridges.

Begin by building relationships in every direction. Up, down, sideways, diagonally; you never know who may become a key ally. As I moved through my career, I made an effort to talk with others to find out what was important to them. I would ask about their challenges and what they wanted to accomplish. And, of course, vice-versa.

These relationships are good things in themselves, but they also give you allies that can help you in many ways:

- If you are pushing for a big change or hunting a big deal, it can be risky for it to be all your own initiative. The more people who are on board with it the better.

- If getting agreement on an action is an uphill climb, you need momentum. That requires having more people in your corner. Maybe some of your colleagues will be in meetings you do not attend, and they can raise the idea there.

- The more widely you can generate enthusiasm for an idea, the more likely it will come to fruition. People will invest in it like it's their own when they are a good ally.

If you are struggling to make things happen, ask yourself: who else can I invite into my canoe to help me paddle?

As a bonus, when you build this kind of trust with many people in your organization, it will be natural for people to see you as a leader when a new position of higher responsibility comes up. You may even have some of your peers automatically suggesting you for a promotion.

LESSON #13: BUILD RELATIONSHIPS

If your goal is to get promoted and reap the rewards, both financial and otherwise, spend time building relationships.

Of course, don't do this in a manipulative "icky" way. Just be proactive in forming genuinely reciprocal relationships. Intentionally look for opportunities to get into conversations with people at all levels of your organization. Talk to them about ordinary, everyday things: their family, what concert they went to last weekend, who won the big game last night. And chat with them about what they are doing at work and what they are trying to accomplish.

Share similar things about yourself when appropriate. When and if the timing is right, many of the relationships will be a natural support to help you move the needle on a big idea.

STOP ASKING FOR PERMISSION

One last piece of advice for making yourself promotable. Once you are in your first leadership position, you need to shift your mindset away from "I'm waiting for someone to tell me what to do." If you are always asking for permission for how to lead your team, the likelihood of a future promotion is low.

As a leader, the organization is now paying you to say "Here's what I see, here's what I am doing, and here's why I'm doing it." By all means communicate it, but not in a way that is looking for permission.

You are being paid to stand on your podium, and like a conductor, see everything (at least in the area you have been assigned). I am not advocating recklessness, of course, but be bold enough to show you are comfortable being decisive and taking responsibility.

CHAPTER 8

TWO PLUS TWO IS....

After 16 years, I left IBM. It was a tough decision. I still look back at the company culture and marvel at the excellence of it, and the amazing people I met and helped me along the way.

However, new opportunities called out to me, and I decided it was time for a new adventure. British Telecom hired me for their Atlanta branch, and after a short time there, they offered me a move to the London office.

Fantastic. That would give me international business experience. Plus, the chance to live for a time in London sounded thrilling. There was just one problem: they weren't actually promoting me, it was a lateral move. As a result, I told the interviewer that the offer to be a sales manager wasn't enough for me to move.

"You can't see the "sales manager" stripe but I already have it," I said, pointing to my arm. "I did that at IBM. I only want to move for a job that is going to stretch me to the next level."

"Okay, great," he replied. "How about we bring you in at the director level and give you profit and loss (P+L) responsibility over your department?"

Done deal. Except now I had to be ready to understand financial reports in a deeper way than I ever had before. It was also kind of a scary jump.

When I first got to London, my fears seemed justified. Early on my boss asked me to update him on the numbers in my department, including monthly trends, how we were performing against budget and against last year, where profit and loss stood currently, etc.

I had no clue what to do. I did, however, have two things going for me. One, I was willing to look foolish and ask for help. And two, there was someone willing to help me. An engineer in my department who knew the ropes explained how to fill in and interpret the financial template I was completing. The result was I found out it was not nearly as complicated as it first seemed. Sure, I had to make an effort, but I was fortunate to have someone patiently explain the concepts, and most of what I learned made sense.

I have discovered over the years that this is usually the way with numbers and financials. They feel forbidding, but when you get right down to it, most of it is simple math, basic concepts, and common sense.

Over the years business owners I have coached like to fall back on "I'm not good with numbers" as an excuse for their lack of financial control of their business. Or they say, "That's why I have an accountant."

My response is always, "What is two plus two?"

"Four" (No one has missed it yet).

"You are good with numbers, then. You just need to understand three basic report cards of a business."

Then I would direct them to Keith Cunningham's terrific book, *The Ultimate Blueprint of an Insanely Successful Business*. Cunningham explains clearly the three report cards and why they matter:

- The Income Statement (this is also sometimes called a Profit & Loss statement or P&L; they are two names for the same thing). This document tracks both revenue and expenses. Many businesses are judging success based on an overemphasis on revenue, without enough account for expenses and net profit.

- The Cash Flow Statement. Many small businesses operate on this metric alone: do I have enough cash right now? They think, "If I have enough cash right now, then I must be doing fine. If I have too little, my business must be doing poorly." Nope. The Cash Flow Statement combined with the other report cards will give you a truer picture AND keep you from running out of cash.

- The Balance Sheet. This helps you track the value of your business. Is your business an asset that is growing and building, or are you essentially an employee that happens to work for yourself?

If you have an accountant or Chief Financial Officer (CFO), you can delegate to them the creation of these reports. You can ask them questions to help you understand them. But under no circumstances should you abdicate your responsibilities to understand your own financials! In short: delegating the creation of your financial reports is fine, but abdicating the analysis of the numbers is never okay.

BOOK RECOMMENDATION:
THE ULTIMATE BLUEPRINT OF AN INSANELY SUCCESSFUL BUSINESS

This book is aimed at entrepreneurs and business owners, and for them I would call this a must read. But if you are a leader with financial oversight of your department, I strongly recommend it as worth your time.

Pay particular attention to page 38. I do not think you could find a better, more succinct explanation of the basic financial documents that every business owner and manager needs to understand. It breaks down how they interrelate with absolute clarity.

If Cunningham can explain financials on one page this simply and this well, there are no excuses left to not know your numbers.

If you were like me in my position in England, you cannot avoid knowing your numbers. I obviously was not the owner or CEO of British Telecom, but I was given the responsibility to manage revenue and expenses within my department. I realized in a sense this was like a mini-CEO job. For anyone learning to move up the ladder, understanding financials is something you need to grapple with sooner or later. Make it sooner.

Another thing this does is keep you grounded when you are suggesting new initiatives. There are many, many ways to drive revenue up. But only some of them make sense from a profitability standpoint. If the expenses necessary to drive the revenue are excessive, you can grow yourself right out of business.

These are the trade-offs that leaders understand, and you need a grasp of these financial basics to understand the choices before you.

BUSINESS OWNERS BEWARE

Late in my career I did a lot of coaching, and many times it involved small business owners. There were some who were waking up late in life to the fact that they did not pay attention to whether they were building assets and value in their business.

There are many smart, passionate people with important ideas and great business missions and they think that is enough. But none of that matters without a grasp of the importance of the numbers. No matter how passionate and beautiful your dreams and hard work, you still can go broke without knowing the impact of your actions to the bottom line.

Often people try stuff that sounds good, but they never actually measure which way that "stuff" is driving the numbers. Going only on your gut is a great way to go out of business fast. Focus on what kind of equity you are building in your business; otherwise, you are simply an employee in your own business.

LESSON #14: BE FINANCIALLY LITERATE

Whether you are a business owner, a mid-level manager, or a high-level executive, you need basic financial literacy.

The one thing a business or department cannot ignore is the bottom line. More precisely, you can only ignore it until it comes back to bite you, and by then it may be too late.

The good news is that none of this will be beyond you if you simply make the effort and are willing to look a little bit foolish at first. Ask good questions, learn, and read Keith Cunningham's book.

CHAPTER 9

EMOTIONAL SOUP

During my time coaching people I noticed many of my clients felt a major objective in life should be the elimination of sadness.

In some ways, that idea makes perfect sense. Feeling sad seems to be blocking more pleasant emotions, and so if we could only get rid of that emotion, we would be happy… right?

There's just one problem. That is not the way emotional intelligence works.

Here is a metaphor for thinking through the role of emotions. Let's say you are making vegetable soup with carrots, green beans, celery, onions, corn, and tomatoes. When you start cooking the soup, the stock begins to boil, and vegetables roll to the surface and then go back under.

Think of the vegetables as representing the range of emotions we feel. Maybe as the soup cooks we enjoy some of the smells of particular vegetables and others we don't.

We might be tempted to turn off the heat if, say, the onions are bothering us as they cook. That would solve one problem, but it would also mean that *all* the vegetables fall to the bottom, even the ones we were most enjoying. And instead of beautiful soup that would have happened if all the flavors had melded together, what you are left with is something less savory and satisfying.

This is also how emotional intelligence and maturity work, too. Trying to pick which of our emotions to favor over others will cut off the beauty of all of them, not just the ones you want to be rid of because they are painful. When feeling pain, we should remember pleasurable emotions, too. We can be present to both the positive and negative emotions, often at the same time. If we are willing to stop and feel our emotions fully, the intensity of pain can also bring an intensity of joy.

This reminds me of an experience after the funeral for my twin brother (I talk more about Stephen in Chapter 13). I vividly recall driving back from that sad event and seeing the incredible beauty of the sunlight on the fields and feeling the music coming from the car stereo in the most intense way. Had I shut down the sad emotions, I would not have felt the intensely joyful ones either.

Sadness is just another emotion you feel, and we cannot cherry pick only the ones we want to feel without doing damage to ourselves. When we try to suppress a legitimate emotion, it will come back to haunt us.

And if you try to push sadness away forcefully, you also suppress your appreciation, your love, your joy, and your happiness, too. It will actually generate more suffering to fail to acknowledge negative emotions. (I should add that you can choose to reject living in a state of suffering, something we will cover in the book's conclusion. This is not the same as trying to suppress sadness).

What does all this have to do with business and leadership? The truth is that emotional maturity and emotional integrity are key skills in business. This becomes kind of obvious when you think about it.

Businesses are made up of people. People sometimes don't get along. Which means inevitably factions form, politics happen, and this can escalate. As a leader, you first need to keep yourself from becoming too deeply identified with emotions you feel.

You will have negative feelings develop toward certain colleagues, or members of your team, or a boss. It's inevitable. The key is to acknowledge them like the onions in the soup without having them take you over or cloud your decision-making.

Leaders also need to keep factions and politics among their team members to a minimum The best ways to do that:

- Be as intentionally even-handed as possible. Remember from Chapter 6 that you always want to use fact-based assessments and not opinions when communicating with team members. That is one of the best ways to stay even-handed.

- Be a leader who models good emotional regulation. This includes not getting too high or too low, but staying focused on what moves the needle.

LESSON #15: MODEL EMOTIONAL INTEGRITY AND MATURITY

Your team looks to you for how to react to the inevitable highs and lows of business. You owe it to yourself and those you lead to work on your emotional maturity. Deal with passing emotions, recognizing them for what they are and not letting them overwhelm you.

You can also show emotional integrity as a leader by always remaining intentionally even-handed. Have objective measurements in place and give team members feedback based on their actions, not on personal likes or dislikes.

Related: See Lesson #11: Make Feedback Specific and Objective. It will give a tremendous boost to your culture and remove unproductive emotions.

KILLING THEM WITH KINDNESS

Here is another way to keep your emotional integrity when dealing with difficult people. Kill them with kindness. This is a good technique if you find yourself actively disliking someone and it is causing turmoil and stealing your focus.

The secret is that it cannot be a brittle, fake kindness. It does not mean you have to like everything about them or all of their behaviors. All you are looking for is something to genuinely like in the other person.

When you are around them, focus on those qualities. You will be amazed that if you do this with sincerity, you will start liking them more. Here is where it gets even more interesting: they will feel that positive vibe. In general, humans naturally reciprocate the emotions and behaviors they are getting from others.

Chances are, if you were having a problem with them, they were having a problem with you. But now, they will feel drawn to like you back. It will confuse them and bug them, but it also will lighten things up between you. Give it a try, you might be surprised by the good things that come out of it.

Note: Be sure to check out Chapter 15 for an even deeper dive on this topic.

Here's another crucial technique for regulating emotions I learned from Tony Robbins. While it might sound small at first, it always worked well for me, and it was very effective with people I coached.

The concept is simple: if you need to have a "Pity Party" for yourself, then have one. We are all human, after all. There is no sense in not acknowledging that we all have tough stuff to deal with at times, or that people sometimes betray us, or that something goes wrong that we didn't foresee… or whatever it is.

The key here is to set a timer for your pity party. Get it out of your system and then move on to actions and emotions that are more productive. A good follow-up to a pity party is to ask yourself, "Okay, I am done with that. Now, what is right about my situation?"

Because while what's wrong is always available, so is what's right. (This is also a concept from Tony Robbins' teachings). The Pity Party is your chance to exorcise what is wrong, and then when it is over, it is time to consciously recognize and choose what is right about the situation.

This is something that I used with my coaching clients all the time. We would get on our call and they would often launch into a litany of negative complaints. I would say, "Oh okay, we're doing this now. That's great. I'm going to set my timer for ten minutes so we'll know when to stop this party." Sometimes they would go ahead and use that time to vent, but oftentimes just saying this snapped them out of their negative state.

LESSON #16: IT'S OKAY TO HAVE A PITY PARTY, JUST SET A TIMER

This one is super simple but incredibly effective. If you have some negativity to let out, do it. If you want to wallow in how you have been victimized by circumstances, people, or plain old bad luck, go for it.

Just set a timer. And when it goes off, ask, "Okay, but what's right about my situation?"

A STORY TO REMEMBER WHEN YOU FEEL LIKE YOU CAN'T CATCH A BREAK

If all else fails, sometimes a joke with a serious point can break us out of our negativity and remind us that things will turn our way again if we keep calm, stay positive, and keep working hard.

Once there were two twin boys who were put in separate rooms as part of a research study. In one room were placed ten toys, the latest and greatest that could be found. The pessimist twin was put in that room and after 30 minutes the researchers returned. The boy told them in detail what was wrong with each of the toys. This one was boring. This one was broken. The batteries died on this one. There wasn't a single toy of the ten that satisfied him.

The other room had a big pile of manure. The researchers put the optimist twin in this room. After 30 minutes, they went in and found this boy shoveling like crazy. The researchers asked what he was doing? "Well with all this manure, there has to be a pony in here somewhere."

I found it helpful on days when nothing was going right, or when a failure happened to remind myself, "Okay, it's time to pull out the shovel. There's got to be a pony here somewhere." Small but simple techniques can keep us sane and moving forward.

CHAPTER 10

HOLDING THE LINE ON CULTURE

A lot of ink has been spilled about how to build a great culture inside a business. There are academic studies galore, and articles about it in publications like Harvard Business Review, and hefty books covering it from every angle.

I don't mean to imply those resources are not valuable. I'm sure there are great things that can be picked up from all of those sources. But a couple of decades ago, I came across a definition of business culture that absolutely nails it, and have never seen anything better since. It is the single most useful description of culture any leader can have. And it is also amazingly concise.

It comes from Chris McGoff's amazing book, *The PRIMES: How Any Group Can Solve Any Problem.* Here it is pictured visually:

Behaviors We Tolerate

_____Culture_____

Behaviors We Do Not Tolerate

At its heart, your culture is the line that defines the behaviors you tolerate and the behaviors you do not. Anything you tolerate is above the line and is considered acceptable. Anything you do not tolerate is below the line, and is not acceptable.

Beautifully simple. But what is not always so simple is having the courage to confront and enforce the standards of culture you claim to want. This definition holds up a mirror to us, showing us what we really allow.

For example, when I was at IBM, gossip was not tolerated. If someone started complaining about a situation behind someone's back, a meeting was called for all the parties involved to confront the problem and resolve it.

As I went to other places on my career journey, I realized that IBM was actually unusual in this. I am sure that if asked, most leaders would say they don't want gossip as a part of their culture. But the truth is, if you tolerate it, then you are saying "yes" to it as a tenet of your culture.

What this points to is the need to call things out and address them when they happen. Many times it is more comfortable to let something go that is sub-par behavior. We all are capable of coming up with plausible sounding excuses as to why it is okay this time. Or we'll just think, "C'mon, it is not that big of a deal."

Okay fine, it is your call as a leader what to address and what to let go. But at least be honest with yourself about what is really going on. Any time you tolerate a behavior, you are validating and confirming it as something that is part of the culture you are building.

There is no wiggle room here. Every single time you praise an action, you are building a culture. Every single time you call out an action for correction, you are building a culture. Every time you silently pass over a negative behavior, you are building a culture. Realize this and be intentional about what you are doing.

LESSON #17: ALWAYS BE MINDFUL OF THE CULTURE YOU ARE BUILDING

There is no more simple or powerful definition of culture than Chris McGoff's: culture is a line, and above it are the behaviors that are tolerated and below it are the behaviors that aren't.

As a leader, all you have to do is encourage the actions that are above the line, and call out the ones that are below it. Any time you are tempted to "let something slide," bring to mind that you are endorsing that behavior as part of the culture.

If you are the leader and you don't like the culture on your team, you need to look in the mirror.

BOOK RECOMMENDATION: *THE PRIMES*

The PRIMES: How Any Group Can Solve Any Problem by Chris McGoff is one of my all-time favorite books. It is more than just about culture, it covers so many topics relevant to business, and it does it so well.

Read this book!

COMMON BEHAVIORS THAT ARE OFTEN TOLERATED THAT SHOULDN'T BE

During my career, I noticed certain common types of unhealthy behavior in many organizations that were often tolerated. Watch out for letting any of these slide:

- Overpaying people without regard to performance.

- Allowing gossip.

- Letting substandard performance get passable reviews.

- Not calling people on deceptions.

- Ignoring chronic lateness.

- Not following through on commitments.

- Not clarifying commitments.
  (Always be sure to specify who is doing what and by when).

In addition, uneven treatment is a killer. If you have a hardworking group but allow one or two people to slack off without correction, what do you think is going to happen? Eventually the hard workers are going to start asking themselves why they bother and less effort will become contagious.

Again, it's very simple. You get what you tolerate.

THE SPECIAL CULTURE AT IBM

At IBM, I was immersed in an excellent culture at the very start of my career. It was not until I experienced other workplaces that I realized just how special it was.

What made it different?

IBM professed some great core beliefs, but many organizations proclaim excellent core values. When I reflect back on it, I think there were two key aspects that elevated IBM culture.

One was a core basic belief proclaimed by IBM: "Respect for the individual." All communications and actions at the company were filtered through the idea that the individual mattered, and was to be respected. This was the baseline.

The other key aspect was that IBM backed up what it professed to believe. The basic beliefs of the company were not something to be posted on the office wall to look nice but then safely ignored.

Here are a few examples:

- At IBM, every manager received 40 hours of training annually on how to lead. Many companies promote someone to a management position and then just let them flounder.

- Every year IBM did a comprehensive survey of its employees. Ten questions were directly related to the performance of their immediate boss. If these surveys showed an issue with the boss and his or her leadership, they were given training and put on notice. Two years of substandard results in this area would usually lead to the person being reassigned to a non-leadership role.

- IBM rewarded its top performers in ways that went above and beyond the norm. They had something called the 100% Club. You got in by nailing or exceeding your expectations for the year. They flew everyone down to the Fontainebleau in Miami. The meals were top notch. The accommodations were first-class. They hired world-famous entertainment talent. It was said if you made the 100% Club your first year, you would never miss again, because you never wanted to be left out of this celebration.

As you build a culture on your own team, it is worth asking two questions:

- How can I respect the people on my team as individuals?

- When we claim to have core values and basic beliefs, how is this being reflected in action?

ADJUSTING TO OTHER CULTURES

While we are on the subject of business and culture, I want to share a couple of small stories about my time in England. If you ever find yourself in an international situation, it is important to be willing to learn other cultural expectations, while still being yourself.

One thing that was interesting in England is that no one talks on elevators. Me, on the other hand, will get on the ground floor with someone and I will be friends with them by the time we are passing the 5th floor. So you could say I kind of stood out in a London elevator. One day a colleague turned to me and asked, "How do you manage to connect like that?" For me it was the belief I mentioned earlier: "A stranger is just a friend I haven't met yet." So even though I was different in this respect, it was tolerated and maybe even slightly admired in some cases.

However, another situation where I did not understand the culture did not work out so well.

It was the end of my first year in London, and I was doing a wrap up meeting. I went around the room and publicly acknowledged something specific that each person had accomplished that year. It was my way of giving some acclamation to everyone on the team, and a way of saying thanks. After the meeting, a senior employee came up to me and said, "Don't ever do that again. That was the single worst thing you can do."

In England, that kind of public praise is an embarrassing social faux paus. I was shocked, because in the United States, we all love praise, acknowledgment, and being called out for something good.

I modified my behavior and never embarrassed people with public praise again.

My larger point is this: if you find yourself in unfamiliar territory, strike a balance between adjusting to other cultures based on respect for other ways of doing things. But don't go so far that you are not yourself. I continued to make friends in elevators!

CHAPTER 11

RUNNING FOR YOUR LIFE

Back in middle school I was a runner and loved being on the track team. Then when I arrived at high school, I was told there was no track team for girls, running not being ladylike enough. I was told gymnastics was the option for young ladies in training.

Ugh.

It is worth mentioning in this context how important Title IX was in expanding opportunities for women and girls in athletics and education. Many people below a certain age don't realize how different it was before this federal civil rights law was passed in 1972. Title IX prohibits sex-based discrimination in any educational program or activity receiving federal financial assistance, and it changed the landscape for young women who wanted to participate in athletics.

Thankfully, the social expectations of the 1960s for "young ladies" are behind us. And also thankfully, I eventually came back to running, and it was never so helpful as when I got promoted to my first leadership role with IBM.

At the time I was working at an IBM office in New Mexico, and had moved into a house a couple of doors down from a colleague. I began running every morning with his wife. A few weeks into our running habit she mentioned that we were on pace to be training for a marathon.

She asked if I had ever run one or even thought about a marathon.

"No, but it sounds like fun. Let's go ahead and do it."

The running was good in itself, of course, but it also had a major benefit for my work life.

This was the first time I was in a leadership position, I was not completely ready for the shift from individual contributor to leader. It was supposed to empower me and put me in charge, but I quickly realized that there were many things that felt outside my control. I could not solely control my performance by my own efforts; I had to motivate others to help me accomplish what needed to be done. So it was a stressful adjustment.

And that's where running provided some saving grace.

Whenever my day went completely sideways, I knew I had achieved one thing: my morning run. At least one good and positive thing was accomplished that day.

It also helped combat my workaholic tendencies. A mentor once told me that I needed to be mindful of this as a leader. If your team sees that you come in super early and stay very late, they feel pressure to match that standard. Without any work-life balance, you will lose some good talent as most people do not want to work to those outsized expectations.

GOING THE DISTANCE

I have found running a particularly good long-term investment in my health and my life. Once I picked up the running habit again in my adult life, I went on to complete 20 marathons, including 13 that helped raise funds for charitable causes I care deeply about.

More recently, it helped when I went to adopt a 5-month old Australian Shepherd dog Ivy from a rescue organization. The agency was hesitant to sign off on the adoption to this retiree. As they put it, "Uh... well... ahem... women your age don't typically adopt high-energy dogs."

I said, "Well, I have trained for and completed 20 marathons in my life, I think I can handle it." This immediately convinced them I was the right choice.

Leaders take care of their health, and it pays off again and again.

Running helped with this, because my morning run pushed back the time to get to the office to something more reasonable. Less time in the office also forces you to figure out how to delegate better instead of trying to do it all yourself. Of course, I am not talking here about seeing how little you can work. I'm simply advocating keeping reasonable hours that will push you to think more strategically about how to get the work done in the allotted time.

Running also helped because it was a physical activity. That relieved stress and provided a healthy contrast to office work. And one more bonus benefit: it was amazing how often the solution to a problem would pop into my mind during a run!

LESSON #18: CONSISTENTLY ACCOMPLISH THINGS OUTSIDE OF WORK

All leaders, but especially newly minted ones, should have something outside of work that gives a sense of pleasure and accomplishment. It should be something that:

- You can do every day (or almost every day) and that gives you at least a small sense of accomplishment.

- Fits around your work schedule, but also forces you to keep less than workaholic hours.

- When possible, do something physical to give your brain a break and keep healthy and energetic.

One other thing to keep in mind: the more stressed we are, the more we are tempted to make the excuse that we don't feel like exercising or that we don't have time for it. That's when you need it the most.

THE MAGIC OF A LIGHT TOUCH

Another great way to battle stress is humor and a light touch. Back when I first got into business, the "tough guy general" was one prominent version of leadership. According to this school of belief, a leader should be George Patton-like, strong-jawed, broad-shouldered, serious, and fearfully authoritative. Almost unapproachable and scary. That ideal is much less believed in today, but I think some of it survives.

Of course, leaders do need to take their responsibilities seriously, and there will always be issues that are no laughing matter. But I have found in my own leadership and observing others that a light touch is more effective than fear and a dour face.

First, look for places that humor fits during the course of conversations. I don't mean coming in with pre-planned jokes or putting together some kind of stand-up routine. When something goes wrong, is there a lighter side to it?

People like to say, "Someday we'll laugh about this" to which the rejoinder should be "Well, then why don't we laugh now?"

Cultivate a lightness of spirit by relating to people. Listen to what they care about, and lend a sympathetic ear, and show empathy while maintaining an emotional equilibrium. It is always a fine balance. You cannot and should not be everybody's best friend, but being over the top with hypermasculinity and fear does not work either.

Here is a thought for reflection: If you make yourself unapproachable, people are going to hide issues from you and you won't know what's going on.

THE "FRIENDS OF BARBARA"

One of the key themes of this chapter is finding things outside of work to keep you balanced. As a leader, the more you can be a well-rounded, emotionally healthy person, the better you will show up each day for your team.

Here's an example from my own life. In 2002, I lost my dear friend Barbara Riefle to cancer. Soon after this loss, I was with several other of Barbara's friends and we were reminiscing about her life and her impact.

As we talked, it became clear that we each thought we had been Barbara's best friend! She had that kind personality. We decided that the connection we were making should not end, and we began meeting regularly, calling our little group "the Friends of Barbara" or the "FOBs." Even as geography and new experiences separated us over the years, we just never stopped connecting faithfully every few weeks.

More than 20 years later, we still meet virtually. (And with today's Zoom technology, it is almost as if we are in the same room!). This support and friendship has been one of the most important parts of my life.

Reflect on this as you get busy and ambitious with your career. Are you taking care to build the kind of relationships that will keep you from burning out? Are you nurturing connections that will keep you emotionally stable so you can be your best self when you show up at the office?

KEEP THE SPOTLIGHT ON YOUR PEOPLE

Another way to keep things in the right spirit at work is to find ways to let your people shine. There are at least two good ways to think about this.

One reminds me of a former boss of mine, Bob Meyers, who was CEO of Millward Brown, a market research firm. When somebody from his team would consult with him about a problem or a new plan, at the end of the conversation he was famous for saying, "I'm sure you'll do the right thing."

He wanted them to own the situation. If there was something in their analysis of the problem that was incomplete, he would ask a strategic question to help illuminate something they might not be seeing.

But overall, Bob was a true CEO who developed other leaders. The spotlight stayed on the other person, while Bob artfully guided them to find their own answers. He trusted his people.

Another aspect of the spotlight is to make sure you do not steal credit or attention away from your team's accomplishments, even if unintentionally.

I stepped directly into this mistake at IBM and it was a lesson I never forgot. We were having a meeting to prepare to announce a new product. As the person running the meeting, I kicked it off with a summary and then turned it over to the systems engineer to fill in the details.

After the meeting the systems engineer made a beeline for my office and came in visibly upset. I was taken aback and had no idea why she was there.

"You stole my thunder," she said. "Your summary gave away all the new information and every key point."

I realized at that moment I had taken the spotlight off one of my team members. To this day I am grateful that she had the courage to come to my office and tell me that it bothered her.

It was a step forward in my evolution as a leader. When you are an individual contributor, you can put the spotlight on yourself when appropriate. Once you become a leader, you should find ways to let your team shine.

LESSON #19: KEEP THE SPOTLIGHT ON YOUR TEAM

A leader develops other leaders, and also inspires them to keep working hard. Keep the spotlight on them in two important ways.

- Show them that you trust them, and then give them specific and objective feedback on their actions and decisions.
- Go out of your way to make sure that they are the ones to shine and get the credit for accomplishments.

Your team will love you for it and stay motivated to work hard.

CHAPTER 12

THE BILLION DOLLAR LESSON

One of the most interesting assignments I had in my career was to find out why Perot Systems lost out on a billion dollars in revenue.

You'll recall from the introduction that I worked for Perot Systems in the 1990s, and Ross Perot told me I delivered the worst presentation he had ever seen. But this was before that presentation. In fact, it was my very first task for Perot Systems.

The company had just lost out on a contract to provide technology services to a major corporation. The contract would have generated $100 million a year in revenue. The length of the contract would have been ten years, so that was a billion dollars of potential revenue that evaporated.

My mission was to find out this: what was the billion dollar lesson. That meant answering the question: What could Perot Systems do to improve its bid process and win the next big opportunity? It is interesting to note that Perot called it a "billion dollar lesson." He instantly put it in terms of the total revenue lost. It wasn't the $100 million lesson (the annual value); it was the entire amount of what could have been won.

I called the organization that rejected our bid and explained what I was doing. You might think that they would not want to be bothered. But not only were they happy to set a meeting with me, the person on the other end of the line seemed intrigued by a business willing to explore their failures. "I don't think we've ever had a vendor come back to us after losing out on a contract to find out why," he told me.

During our meeting, he pulled out his organization's Request for Proposal (RFP) and pointed to a question in it. Then he pulled out the Perot Systems' proposal. Then he said, "Show me in the proposal where that question was answered."

I read the proposal, and saw his point. There may have been a faint answer buried somewhere in it but if so, it was too convoluted to find easily. While the proposal was detailed, and showed hard work had been put into it, we had missed the bigger picture. We failed to give simple clear answers to the big questions in the RFP. Instead we described every tree and lost sight of the forest.

That was not the only thing I discovered during my investigation. It turned out that the winning bidder had a connection with someone on the organization's board. To put it plainly, one of the decision-makers had a financial reason for choosing another company.

So the other key takeaway: we didn't do our due diligence on the makeup of the board of directors, the ones who would make this huge decision.

Had we known that early on, we could have:

- Decided not to proceed and spend all the time and investment to enter into the bid process we had little to no chance of winning because of another company's advantage.

- Told the prospective client we knew about the competitor's connection to one of their board members, and ask for assurance that would not disadvantage our bid.

The analysis produced two clear lessons for improving our bid process. One, we formed a committee to review all bids to make sure that all questions in an RFP were answered clearly and directly.

Also, we added items to the checklist for analyzing any prospective bid. Among them: who are the decision-makers, what is their background, what do they care about, and do we have a fair shot?

There are so many great things to pull out of this story.

Businesses take credit for wins and celebrate them, and rightly so. But when they lose, the prospect is blamed for making a bad decision. Or sometimes we blame the competition for undercutting us, or the business climate, or whatever reasons are handy. And then we leave it at that, and on we go.

That reminds me of one of my favorite mantras: The only time you fail is when you fail to learn. There is no need to hide from failure, because there is no such thing if you treat it as a learning lesson. As I said before, success is actually boring; it is the failures that are interesting!

Perot Systems did not send a senior executive to find out what happened. They sent me, a recent hire without preconceived biases or an interest in creating an excuse – I hadn't been there when it happened. It was a commitment to truly learn and a genuine curiosity.

Another lesson is that thanks to what we learned, actual changes were made and systematized. How many times do we know the changes that need to be made, but never actually make them? Many businesses lack this discipline for follow-through. If you see the same mistakes being made over and over, this is a sure sign that you need to up your leadership game.

LESSON #20: LEARN FROM SETBACKS AND THEN MAKE CHANGE HAPPEN

I'll say it again because it is such an important mantra: the only time you fail is when you fail to learn. Another pithy way to say it: Reflect, don't deflect.

- Do not wallow in "poor me" emotions after a setback.

- Do not make excuses, even ones that are legitimate.

- Do not brush off setbacks or sweep them under the rug.

Analyze. Figure out where it went wrong, and how next time can be different. Don't forget to look at what was right, too, so you can also retain and build on that.

Finally, don't let your lesson go to waste by letting the team (and yourself) slip back into the same old habits and processes. What practically can you do with the lesson you learn? And how can you systematize it to make it stick?

This is one of the most important lessons in this book. When you master it, your leadership will take a huge leap forward.

GHOST THE OBJECTION

Of course, sometimes the best way to deal with failure is to figure out ways to prevent it in the first place. There's a venerable sales technique called "ghost the objection" which can help us see how to do this.

The idea in sales is that you figure out in advance the possible objections a prospect might have about what you are selling and you address those concerns before they ask the question.

You build into the presentation the answer to the objections, and it sends the message to your prospects that you have taken the time to think through how this may impact them. One useful way to do this is to use a pre-frame. This is something you do right up front so the objection is not nagging inside your audience's head.

For example, maybe your client is in year seven of a ten-year contract with you, and you are trying to sell them on an early renewal. They are thinking the whole time, "We still have three years to go, why would we be talking about this now?"

In this scenario, you immediately let them know the incentive you are offering for renewing now, and why it is more advantageous than in three years. Pre-frame the whole conversation with this right off the bat.

You can probably see the benefits of this for sales, but it can be as helpful in almost any business situation. If you have a presentation coming up to senior executives, what question do you most dread them asking? Anticipate it and have an answer ready, or even build in the answer.

Or maybe you have to announce what you know will be an unpopular new company policy to your team. How can you anticipate what they will object to, and how can you best build your response in your announcement?

"KNOW YOUR STUFF"

Having a complete grasp of what you are selling or presenting is something for which to strive. One time when I was with IBM I was in front of a group selling a particularly complex piece of technology and I could see my audience was getting a little bored and antsy. So I decided to switch things up.

I announced we would play "Stump the Stars." I said, "What frustrations do you have that you want this system to be able to solve? Ask me anything and we'll see how it works." As they fired off requests, I demonstrated how it would work on the system. And by turning the product demonstration into a game, it made it a lot of fun and became super engaging for everyone in the room.

What gave me the confidence to do this was my thorough knowledge of the technology I was selling (and its superiority). In other words, one of the best ways to anticipate is to "know your stuff" so thoroughly that you can't be stumped.

HANDLE SURPRISE

One final tip: Despite the best laid plans, sometimes you get a question or objection you do not anticipate.

If you don't know or if you are unsure of how to respond, don't say what most people say, which is "I don't know, but…" Instead, say, "I'm really glad you asked that because it gives me an opportunity to talk about…"

This way of phrasing does a few things:

- It buys you a little extra time. In that little gap you've opened up, you will think of something. It becomes a cue for your brain to generate an answer. I have personally found that it always does.

- It aligns you with the questioner instead of making them an adversary. ("I'm really glad you asked that…").

- By calling it an "opportunity," you are phrasing it as something positive.

In summary, when you are preparing a message or presentation, think through objections, know your stuff, and if all else fails, buy yourself a little breathing room by being really glad someone asked that question.

CHAPTER 13

THE POWER OF QUESTIONS

One of my hopes for this book is that the lessons you learn in it will not just make you a better leader, but will also improve your life. Lessons learned in a career can also carry over to have remarkable impact in all areas of your life.

I was reminded of this when I was driving my twin brother Stephen to a doctor's appointment. Diagnosed with terminal liver cancer, he had very little time left.

Back then I was training to be a coach with Robbins Research International, a Tony Robbins' company.

As we drove along, Stephen asked, "So what are you learning in your coach training?"

I told him one of the things I was learning was about the power of questions. I shared how questions are a great way to engage with people. They work best when you give short answers to people, stop talking, and then let them ask another question.

And then I practiced what I was preaching by clamping my mouth shut. My brother would ask more if he wanted to know more.

After a moment, he asked, "Well, can you give me an example of how it works?"

"Well, with what you are going through right now, you could ask, 'What's great about this situation?'" I wanted to say more, but I knew I needed to discipline myself and not take over the conversation by answering my own question.

He sat quietly for a good while, and I could tell he was thinking and thinking. Finally, he said, "I can't think of one great thing about terminal cancer."

Again, I fought the temptation to tell him my answer. I knew that the power of questions and dialogue would be more effective, and more respectful of him as a partner in the conversation. I simply said, "I understand. It took me a long time to come up with what is great about this situation."

Another pause, and then Stephen asked, "Well, what did you come up with?"

"Well, what's great about this situation is that you didn't just wake up dead one morning like our dad did. We have all this time to talk."

He burst out laughing. Because I had given him all this time to process it in a paced dialogue of questions, he saw the humor in it. But he also saw some truth in what I was saying.

He agreed that it was great that we had time to talk.

And my next question was, "So what do you want to talk about?"

That led into an exceptionally heartfelt and connecting conversation. We even had the courage to talk about his memorial, including a joke he wanted included (a request I honored a few months later). This drive to the doctor together was one of the most meaningful and memorable moments of my life.

And it happened, at least in part, because I had learned the power of questions. Of course, this was a particularly charged example of it, but it is useful every day, from the ordinary to the extraordinary.

I need to take one step back here and provide one more piece of context.

Around this time, I was also learning about VAK learning styles. VAK represents three different ways we process the world: V = visual, A = auditory, and K = kinesthetic. With VAK, learners are categorized by the primary way they take in information. (Some people combine these styles, but for most, one is dominant).

Visual learners learn best through sight; those who do it through sound are auditory learners, and kinesthetic learners take in information from movements or by doing.

As I thought these categories through, I realized that I am a visual learner and Stephen was a kinesthetic learner. This made using questions and back and forth even more important. Visual learners tend toward talking too much, and kinesthetic learners are more quiet and reflective. If I did not restrain myself, I would want to provide all the answers instead of listening to Stephen.

This point is important for leaders to grasp. Since there are multiple ways to learn, and because we process information differently and at different rates, using questions and dialogue is a superior form of communication.

LESSON #21: USE THE POWER OF QUESTIONS FOR MORE EFFECTIVE COMMUNICATION

As a leader, it is tempting to want to dominate to get your point across. Or to feel pressure to have all the answers.

A much better and more effective approach is to rely on the power of questions. Even when you think you have the right answer. Especially when you think you have the right answer.

Enter into a genuine dialogue and learn to not try to say everything. Instead, say something, preferably a question, and then stop. If the other person wants more information, they'll say so. Leave in pauses for people to process information.

This is especially important because not everyone has the same communication and learning styles and skills. Opening up a dialogue instead of a "bossy" monologue is more effective.

Using questions at the proper time and pace makes others an equal part of the dialogue. Questions are an invitation to others.

GOOD QUESTIONS & BAD QUESTIONS

Whenever I would visit my mother's house, I always picked the same coffee cup from her cupboard to use. On its side was a frame from the long running cartoon strip "Shoe" by artist Jeff MacNelly.

The cartoon's tagline is, "If you don't know the answer, question the question." I always loved this bit of wisdom. It gets at what we should do when we don't have all the answers. Start again with questions.

But some questions work better than others, especially if you are seeking answers to problems and issues. As a rule of thumb, open-ended questions that encourage dialogue and express curiosity are more effective. These are questions that start with Who, What, When, and Where. On the other hand, questions that start with Why can be much less effective (with one exception that I will get to in a moment).

Let's look at two examples from the world of personal development and business. Let's say the issue is: I need to lose weight or I need to improve my sales results.

If you start with a Why question, it becomes "Why haven't I been able to lose weight?" Or "Why haven't I been able to generate more sales?"

Answers to these kinds of questions tend to be narratives that seek to explain instead of usefully analyzing the problem. They also often tend toward unhelpfully accusatory language (either directed at ourselves or others).

In this case, the answer might be: "Because I have no self-control and I'm completely addicted to chocolate." Or "they aren't buying my product because I'm not good enough, I don't know enough or I'm not disciplined enough."

Notice how starting down the Why path creates a narrative with a reason/excuse that cannot be overcome, or only overcome with white knuckle willpower. "Why answers" tend to go in the direction of supposed character traits that cannot be changed.

So change it up. Stop asking why. Think about questions like this instead:

- What can I do to lose weight? What can I do to sell more?

- What have I done in the past that worked?

- Who can I make an ally in losing weight? Who are the best sales people I could learn from?

- Where can I go to lose weight or learn advanced sales skills?

- What are strategies I can use to lose weight? What are sales strategies I'm not using?

- What resources are available?

- What will my life be like when I've reached my ideal weight or reach my sales goals?

Answers to those types of questions generate practical, specific actions you can move forward with. They keep you out of a storytelling mode that could lead you to beat yourself up (or blame somebody else).

As a leader, one of the ultimate shut down questions is "Why did you do that?" That is not opening up a dialogue; it is an accusation. Again, it is better to rely on What, Who, Where and When.

- What was the thinking behind this decision?

- Where were you hoping this would go?

- Who else did you involve?

- Where can we go from here?

- What happened that led to this?

These questions explore practical lessons and think through ways to mitigate what has already happened. They lead to thinking about the future instead of dwelling on the past.

Another great question approach is a "How" question. If you are stuck with a problem, or just need to brainstorm other pathways, ask this very illuminating question: "How else can we get this done?" Pull that out when nothing else seems to be working.

Okay, now it is time to give "Why" questions some props, because there are times when it is incredibly useful.

Why questions are good for looking forward and discovering your motivation. Let's go back to the original examples. Say you are still looking to lose some weight or increase your sales results. The helpful Why question to ask is "Why is this important to you?"

Answers to these kinds of questions create leverage on yourself and others. They remind you of the whole point behind what you are doing. Without the answer to forward-looking Why questions, we'd never get off the couch. So don't use Why to biopsy the past; use it to fuel the future.

One final thought: Be thoughtful with your questions and use the "less is more" approach when asking them. Don't just spew random questions or you will seem like a prosecutor questioning a hostile witness.

One excellent way to become better at only asking the best and most incisive questions is to pay close attention to the questions great leaders ask. I always played a game with myself to try to guess what a leader would ask. Say a leader is in a meeting going over a 50-page brief with the team. What questions does she ask that no one else is? Learn from the best.

LESSON #22: ASK THE MOST EFFECTIVE QUESTIONS

Ask questions that generate practical answers that help, not narratives that don't. In general, ask Who, What, Where, and When questions and stay away from Why questions.

Only ask Why questions as fuel for the future, to discover your fundamental motivations for action.

Also, pay attention to the questions you are selecting. Are you choosing the most effective question for the moment, or are you piling on question after question without much thought?

Great leaders ask great questions. Focus on getting better at this skill.

CHAPTER 14

CLIMBING THE MOUNTAIN ONE STEP AT A TIME

One particularly memorable senior leader from my time at IBM was my boss, Chappy Maxwell, the head of the training center in Atlanta. As his insights accumulated along with his years, he would discover another piece of wisdom that he would formulate into a maxim. If it was useful enough, he would number it and add it to a list he called Maxwell's Laws.

One of those laws was: "Beware of the parabolic nature of a career path."

A parabola is a mathematical term that describes a curve on a graph. On each side of the graph, the curve is a mirror image of the other side. Put another way: when the ascent is steep on one side, the descent will be equally steep on the other.

Of course, Chappy was warning that too fast a climb up the career ladder will most likely lead to a spectacular fall in the not-too-distant future.

Chappy advocated a steady, intentional growth in skills and responsibilities. This is what builds a career that lasts. If you get a promotion that is a huge percentage bump in salary or responsibility or both, then the odds of failure go way up. It is great to have ambition, but it is wise to temper it with good judgment.

In my own career, I followed a pattern of starting with the core necessary skills for a position, but also gaining another crucial skill that would allow me to stretch to a new level.

A few examples of what I mean:

- At IBM, I came in with a good foundation of sales skills, and then I learned the technology so I had an area of expertise. This gave me the core familiarity I needed with the company and its products, and then I was promoted to a series of leadership positions that added that core skill.

- At British Telecom, I had a chance to accept a lateral move to a sales leadership position in London, but I insisted on more because I already had that core skill. I got promoted to director-level and stretched to understand the financial reports and had profit and loss responsibility.

- Skipping to the end, all the skills I built at each level and each new position all came together in a capstone that allowed me to execute on my dream job as the Director of Coaching for Robbins Research International. Of course, I did not know that such a job existed or that it would be where all my skills would point me at the beginning of my career. You have to build a step at a time and you might be pleasantly surprised by where it takes you.

What you want to avoid, or at least question thoroughly, is an opportunity that sounds too good to be true. If someone is offering to double or triple your salary for a new job or promotion, what are the expectations that will come along with this? No one hands you more money or responsibility for no reason. They are going to expect double or triple the value. Will that be realistic for your current skill level?

I remember somebody leaving one of my organizations for a huge jump in salary and position elsewhere. I thought to myself as it was happening, "I don't think he is ready for that." And, unfortunately, I heard six months later that he was looking for work again.

A great question to ask during an interview for a job or promotion of your prospective boss is:

"If you do bring me on board, imagine it is 12 months from now. What have I accomplished that makes you thrilled you hired me?"

If they cannot answer this with any kind of clarity, run. If they answer with outlandish expectations, run. Any leader who cannot answer this with clear and reasonable expectations does not know what they are doing and you should not trust your career with them.

LESSON #23: BUILD YOUR CAREER IN THOUGHTFUL STEPS

Treat your career with the big picture in mind. Where do you want to go ultimately? What skills do you need to add to get there?

How can you leverage core skills you have now to get a promotion, while also knowing that the new position will stretch you to add another skill?

Career paths won't always be a straight line, and we cannot control everything that happens. But we should at least intentionally think through any potential move up the ladder.

Build your career with intention, and don't make money or title the sole reason for accepting a promotion. Those are factors, but should not be the only basis.

Above all, make sure the next move does not come with outlandish expectations from an unrealistic boss. Always remember to ask, "Imagine it is 12 months from now. What have I accomplished in that time to make you thrilled you hired me?"

BUT ALSO, DON'T BE TOO CAREFUL

It is important to be clear that none of what I've discussed in this chapter should scare you from taking leaps. The best career moves I have made have all scared the heck out of me one way or the other.

I remember when I first got a great job with Millward Brown as the Chief Talent Officer, I was terrified to go in on my first day, and I had to force myself to go in. I did not have the background or degrees that most HR leaders did. Who did I think I would fool trying to do this job? In fairness, I did ask Bob Meyers why he was hiring me for the Chief Talent Officer role. He said that I had a background in training and recruitment, and that the local HR teams could handle the daily responsibilities.

If you are unsure of your ability, recall that if someone is willing to hire or promote you, they think you can do it. Again, as long as you have tested their expectations to make sure they are not ridiculous, you will likely succeed with hard work. It also doesn't hurt to invest in leveling up your skills with education. Once I was in this role, I did earn my Senior Professional in Human Resources (SPHR) certification so that I could appreciate what the local HR teams were doing.

Also, keep in mind that everyone suffers from Imposter Syndrome sometimes. We all feel like we are faking it when something happens that we do not have an answer to or where we suffer a big disappointment. Situations like this call for what I said in the introduction: Get curious. Learn from failure (and then it's not failure). The best cure for Imposter Syndrome is to stop worrying about your ego and start getting curious.

YES... WE ALL FEEL LIKE IMPOSTERS
A LOT OF THE TIME

Something interesting happened when I sent the original draft of this book out to mentors and colleagues for feedback. More than one of them specifically mentioned Imposter Syndrome and how they had struggled with it many times throughout their careers.

What surprised me most was that when I worked with them, I never would have guessed they felt that way.

It just goes to show how common these feelings are—even among people we admire and look up to. If you're ever tempted to feel like you're the only one who struggles with this, you're not. Imposter Syndrome is something we can all push through.

Finally, if you cannot decide whether you are making too big a leap or are just playing it too safe, the answer is probably, "Go for it." You will either make a mistake and learn from it, or succeed and be thrilled.

THE PROBLEM MIGHT JUST BE... YOU

After 37 years in business, I was "downsized" due to a corporate reorganization. How could this be happening? After all the hard work I had invested in my career, why was it coming to this? It was so unfair.

My work situation had radically changed through circumstances not of my doing. I was getting shut out of important communications and I was having very negative thoughts toward a key person in my work life. I did not seem part of the vision going forward.

This had been going on for some time, and my sadness and resentment was building. There did not seem to be any way out.

I was hitting emotional rock bottom one night during a business trip in a New York City hotel room. I couldn't sleep and it was 2 am. I was mindlessly flipping channels while negatively obsessing about the whole situation.

I stopped on one channel. This was the height of the time of infomercials, where products and services were advertised for 30 or 60 minutes, and you could call a number to order whatever they were selling.

This one was for a Tony Robbins product called Ultimate Edge. I was somewhat familiar with Tony because I had listened to some of his tapes in the 1970s. This was a re-introduction to him, and the product was intriguing. But what got me to pick up the phone was the bonus offer for a free session with a Robbins' coach. I could not dial fast enough.

At this point, I knew I needed something to seriously change my trajectory. That offer of a free coaching session was a lifeline and I felt some hope and excitement for the first time in months.

As it would turn out, I was right to sense a big turnaround. The lowest point of my career would push me to call, and that call would eventually lead to the biggest success of my career. But I'm getting ahead of my story.

For now, I had my free coaching session and that was my focus. I kind of imagined this like that famous scene in the movie *Indiana Jones & The Last Crusade*. Indiana comes to a chasm and he cannot see the bridge across it until he takes the first step. This reaching out felt like that kind of leap of faith for me.

I went on to hire this coach after the first session, and to this day I am grateful for Cindy Rold. The truth is I was pretty bitter at that time, and she was a fantastic angel who appeared in my life.

Right from the get-go, she introduced me to what became a foundational exercise for me. It was created by Byron Katie, and is still available on her website, thework.com. The exercise is called the "Judge Your Neighbor" worksheet, and it is part of what Katie calls "The Work."

BOOK RECOMMENDATION: *LOVING WHAT IS: FOUR QUESTIONS THAT CAN CHANGE YOUR LIFE*

The four questions on the Judge Your Neighbor worksheet are explored in a deeper way in the book, Loving What Is by Byron Katie. She shows you how to radically change the dynamic in relationships and situations where you are suffering.

I *highly* recommend this book for getting down to the core of how your thoughts connect with suffering, and how to free yourself.

I recommend visiting her website to download it to do the full exercise. Here is a condensed version of how it works. First, start with your thought about another person (the one you are having a problem with). Then ask:

- Is it (my thought) true?
- Can you absolutely know it is true?
- How do you react when you believe that thought?
- Who would you be without that thought?

And turn it around and find 3 genuine examples of how it might be true in your life. (Meaning, how you do the same thing that you are judging your neighbor for.)

It is important that you take the time to sit and write all this out. The exercise will not be effective if you only try to think it through in your head.

Here is a slimmed-down example of how this could work:

Negative thought toward the other person: This person isn't updating me on what is going on and is freezing me out of important communications.

Is this thought true (Yes or No)?

• Yes.

Can you absolutely know it is true (Yes or No)?

• No.

How do you react, what happens, when you believe that thought?

• I become sad and bitter.

Who or what would you be without the thought?

• Well, I certainly wouldn't be upset and bitter if it wasn't true that I was being left out by this person.

And now the turnaround: Find 3 ways that I am not updating people as much as I should be.

Answering this question forces you to see that most of the time we get back what we give, and that our own way of behaving is having an impact on how we perceive things.

This was so valuable in pulling me out of my tailspin toward the other person. However, I do not want to give the impression that it is always easy or fast. My coach assigned me this worksheet four weeks in a row until I finally had a breakthrough. I kept writing it out, and eventually I could see how I was doing the same thing. I wasn't communicating enough, I was closing myself off, and then I changed my behavior.

I changed the dynamic of how I dealt with this person, and eventually we became allies. But even more than the outward change, it was the internal mental release and freedom from my resentment that was the real win. And it all came from good coaching.

That was to be a sign for my future.

LESSON #24: FIND A WAY TO FREE YOURSELF FROM NEGATIVE DYNAMICS WITH OTHERS

When we get caught up in deeply negative ways of relating with others, the person we hurt most is ourselves. Even when we know that we need a way out, it can be hard to accept and find a different path.

"The Work" at Byron Katie's website is a proven way to find that path. It reveals that our thoughts generate the suffering. Those thoughts also generate our own behaviors, which are then mirrored back to us.

If you find yourself in a situation where you feel unfairly treated, victimized, and you are sure everyone else is to blame, give the Judge Your Neighbor worksheet and The Work a try. It will restore your freedom and power back to you.

Note: Don't think of this worksheet as only for dealing with a difficult situation with a boss. It works with colleagues, direct reports, and personal relationships.

Here is another related technique you can use. Take out a sheet of paper and write out a description of any person you are upset with. Get it all out. "He/she did this, he/she did that."

Once you are done, scratch out all the "he/she" words and write in "I." Then reflect. This forces you to acknowledge your role in the drama. The more you can do exercises like this, the more you grab back your own power.

All of this reminds me of another saying of Tony Robbins. I referenced it earlier, but here it is in the full context: "Life is simple. Everything happens for you, not to you. Everything happens at exactly the right moment, neither too soon, nor too late."

How can you get to a place where you see this is true, even when it feels like bad things are happening to you? It is as simple and hard as this: Believe and understand that adversity is happening for your development. And that does not mean that in the moment your emotions are happy about how the progress is being made. But nonetheless, it is still happening for you.

NOTE: There may be times that you will not be able to pull yourself out of a negative situation all on your own. Without coaching at the right time in my life, I would not have been able to make the many of the leaps I did. For more on when and how to hire a coach, see Appendix 1.

CHAPTER 16

THE PEOPLE YOU WANT WORKING FOR YOU... AND THE PEOPLE YOU DON'T

I had a brief stint later in my career as an executive recruiter. The whole job focused on helping companies find great talent, and it gave me a chance to interview tons of people. That kind of concentrated experience can help you to refine your skills quickly.

Around this time I was reading M. Scott Peck's classic book, *The Road Less Traveled*. The book covers a lot of ground on a lot of topics, and is well worth reading for many reasons. One of the themes is that there are some people who are very resistant to change, and it is very hard to get past that because the root problem is they won't take responsibility for their actions.

It struck me that Peck's insight was true of my experience in the workplace. You can basically put people into two buckets: Those who take responsibility and those who do not.

And the key to a great team is to fill it with people who take responsibility. These are people who will grow right along with you. The ones that don't take responsibility stay stagnant and are difficult to work with or change. They are always deflecting instead of learning. It's the economy, it's the other guy, it's that circumstance, and on and on.

When interviewing someone, how do you determine the difference? Everybody is in their best clothes, their shoes are shined, and they have on their game face. It can be hard to break through the façade and get to the truth of who they are and how they will work.

BOOK RECOMMENDATION:
THE ROAD LESS TRAVELED

This book by a then little-known psychiatrist named M. Scott Peck was published in 1978. You might say it took a while for the word to get out: the book did not hit the bestseller list for six years. But once enough people read it, it took off because of its great wisdom and has sold more than ten million copies.

Peck shares many important insights into discipline, love, and suffering. For leaders, one of the big lessons is that people will remain resistant to change unless they take responsibility for their actions.

I came up with a "secret weapon" strategy to figure this out. I have conducted several thousand interviews, so this is definitely battle-tested. I have never before talked about this technique except with a small circle of people.

It is very effective, and I highly recommend it if you need to add people to your team. Here is how it works:

Midway through the interview I would ask, "What has been your greatest accomplishment in your career?"

People love to talk about their successes, and I usually would get an expansive answer. The interviewee was then in a relaxed frame of mind, with their guard down a little bit.

Then I would immediately follow it up with this question: "What has been your greatest disappointment in your career?" The key here is not the disappointment itself; that is almost irrelevant.

Once they identified what it was, I asked a simple two-word question, "What happened?" And then I paid rapt attention to their answer.

Some people say things like: "Wow, I just didn't anticipate X" or "What I learned was Y" or some other statement where they take responsibility in the form of an "I" statement.

Other people will answer by saying things like, "They changed the bonus plan halfway through the year…" or "They tied one hand behind my back and so…" or some other reason that put the responsibility on "they" or some other outside influence.

Those that fell into the second camp I immediately eliminated from consideration and found a way to gracefully end the interview. You only want to consider people who are all-in on taking responsibility for what happens.

This is so important from a leadership perspective. A huge percentage of your success is dependent on the quality of your team. If someone joins who is a weak link, it can be challenging to get rid of them, not to mention all the time wasted dealing with it. Holding them accountable and building up a case for their departure is even tougher because they are always deflecting.

On the other hand, those who step up and take responsibility learn the fastest, complain much less, and make you look good.

A JOKE WITH A SERIOUS POINT:
THE TOWN COP AND THE OUT-OF-TOWNERS

In a small town, there was a local police officer known for pulling over out-of-state cars — not for speeding, but just as they were entering town.

Each time, he'd ask the driver, "So, what brings you to our little town?"

Often, the reply was, "We were thinking about moving here."

The officer would nod, lean in, and ask, "What is it like where you are from?"

If they said, "We're from a great town. People are friendly, the schools are good, and it's a nice place to live," the cop would smile and say, "You'll love it here — folks are just the same."

But if they said, "We're from a terrible town. People are rude, nothing ever works, and everyone's out for themselves," the cop would shake his head and say, "Well, I'm sorry to say it's pretty much the same around here."

This parable perfectly captures the point. People's attitude shapes their perception. If you have people on your team who always "live in a terrible town," your team is in trouble.

LESSON #25: ADD TO YOUR TEAM WITH CARE AND INTENTION

With a weak team, you cannot succeed as a leader. It is absolutely crucial that you find and add the right people. The best foundation is to get people on your team who take responsibility and avoid those who don't.

Use the interview sequence outlined above as a guide for hiring the right people. You will be amazed at how well it works in revealing the fundamental orientation of a prospective hire.

Very few things will be as important as how you build your team, so take this lesson to heart.

HOW NOT TO IMPROVE YOUR TEAM

If you are a leader with someone underperforming, figure out why. Are they unwilling to take responsibility; is it a mismatch between roles and skills; or is it a lack of quality feedback (the person does not know what they are doing wrong)?

If it is the lack of quality feedback, revisit Chapter 6. If it is a mismatch between roles and skills, do they have the ability to level up the skills? If so, help them get there.

If it is an unwillingness to take responsibility, or if it just does not match their skill set, you need to let them go (following the proper processes of your workplace, of course).

One temptation is not to fire them, but instead help them get hired elsewhere in your organization. Don't do it. If you are asked by a colleague about them, you need to give a full picture. Disclose what the team member is good at and where they are weak.

While it can feel good to get rid of a problem person, when you pass them off within the company you are doing long-term damage to your reputation. You will be known as someone untrustworthy, someone who chooses their own benefit over the good of the company.

One time at IBM I was put in charge of a team and could see that one person was struggling in several important areas. I was also told that I would never be able to get rid of him because he was so good in one particular area.

It kept his ratings up high enough that I was supposed to overlook the rest. After a time, I realized what he was best at was presentations, and that our audience of sales trainees loved his speeches.

Eventually I had a conversation with him and the upshot was that he knew he was weak in many of the other areas and wasn't happy about that either. As we discussed it further, it became clear that his talent and his dreams were to give motivational speeches full-time.

"Then why don't you do that?" I asked. Within a short period of time, he was able to leave and went on to find wonderful success doing something he loved. He would later send me a piece of the Berlin Wall after it fell in 1989 to thank me for helping him see a different way forward.

Sometimes all people need is someone to help them figure out that their happiness and success lies elsewhere.

CHAPTER 17

WHEN TO SHIFT INTO NEUTRAL

We all would like to think our career will be one long chain of going from strength to strength. Of course, we know there will be some ups and downs, but we also would like to believe that hard work will keep us from ever facing the kind of serious setback that makes us question everything.

That has not been my experience, or the experience of most people I know. As the old saying has it, "The only thing you can count on is change."

- Maybe it is a reorganization or a change of leadership.

- Maybe your company decides to cease operations in your location or ceases altogether.

- Or maybe you will just one day realize that you are not having fun anymore and that you have grown dissatisfied.

Any or all of those can happen. I know first-hand.

And what do many of us do? We seek an *immediate* solution. In the United States in particular, we tend toward a ready-fire-aim mentality. It often serves us well, but when a big change is called for, it may not be the right approach.

Soon after I started being coached, I became completely intrigued by the idea of coaching. I began to wonder if this is what I should be doing next? It certainly seemed like the right move. That motivated me to enroll in a coaching certificate program at Columbia University to learn more.

One of the books on the reading list was *Transitions: Making Sense of Life's Changes* by William Bridges. It opened my eyes to the value of the neutral zone.

According to Bridges, a major life change will go through three stages. Stage 1 is that something sparks the need for a change. Maybe it is something that comes from outside you and forces you to make a major life move. Loss of job, a key relationship ends, or some other major external change. Or maybe it is coming from internal drives. Whatever the case, it is time for a big change.

Here is where our rushed mentality can push us into a place of suffering and confusion. In America, we are often closely identified with our job. Socially, it can feel like you are not much without one. When something forces or sparks a change, we want to solve it right now.

What Bridges says is spend some time in Stage 2, what he calls the Neutral Zone.

This is a place between old and new, a no man's land where the old reality is gone but the new is not clear yet.

What Bridges advocates is not to fight the confusion. There is a beauty to being willing to stay in the neutral zone. It will be a time of creativity, renewal, and development. One of the challenges for most people going through the neutral zone is that they expect to understand it. We want there to be a straight line from old to new.

BOOK RECOMMENDATION: *TRANSITIONS*

The time will come in your life or career where major change comes in and knocks you for a loop. Or you force a major shift on your own because you know you need it.

That would be a good time to get yourself a copy of *Transitions: Making Sense of Life's Changes* by William Bridges. It will help you see that change that impacts your identity is not a surface thing, and that it takes time.

You need to be okay with confusion and slowing down enough to give the quiet but deep voice in you a chance to speak.

Eventually, Stage 3 happens, where you find your way out of it and things become clearer. The way I like to think of it is this: Stay quiet enough in yourself to hear the whispers of destiny. This goes all the way back to Lesson #1, Have the Courage to Change.

When I was starting out in life and I realized that I enjoyed my night waitressing job better than my "real" job for which I had gone to college, it was tough. But I could not ignore my inner voice and eventually I knew I had to make a change.

When I was struggling at the low point of my career, coaching came into my life. It was something I had never considered before, but again, the whispers of destiny came in and began to point me in a new direction. As I'll share in the next chapter, that new direction was absolutely life changing.

LESSON #26: WHEN BIG CHANGE HAPPENS, SPEND SOME TIME IN THE NEUTRAL ZONE

When circumstances or destiny push you into a major life or career shift, resist charging full speed ahead. Spend some time reflecting, renewing, and recharging.

Do not expect time in the neutral zone to be a straight line or completely logical. Do not expect it to be a time when you have 100 percent clarity on where you will end up. Trust that you will find your way.

Have enough inner calm to be able to listen to the whispers of destiny. Eventually you will see the path forward, and you'll be grateful that you stayed in the neutral zone long enough to figure it out.

CHAPTER 18

COACHING ISN'T ABOUT YOU

A few chapters back, I shared the story of the lowest point of my career. At that moment, I dialed in from a New York City hotel room to buy a personal development product and a free session with a Tony Robbins' coach.

As my coach helped me figure a way out of my funk, I became more and more fascinated by coaching. I was able to get in the program at Columbia University, and did some coaching within the corporate environment. But I was edging toward something new. I was reflecting on whether to become a trained coach in the Tony Robbins organization.

It is easy to forget because now coaches are everywhere, but Tony essentially invented the coaching industry in the early 2000s. He and his organization were the gold standard for coaching (and in my mind still are). I thought, "If I'm going to go all-in on becoming a coach, that is where I want to be."

But I am also a big believer in doing my due diligence, and I wanted to know more before jumping in head first.

After I worked with my coach for about six months, I decided to attend a Robbins seminar called Business Mastery. This was a five-day investment of time and resources. But I wanted to get a real feel for the teachings, and so I went with this immersive experience. This put me closer to a decision because I got so much value out of the seminar. I remember thinking, "I could work with this person, this could be my next career move."

But I still wanted to know more. I wanted to make sure that Tony was as authentic off stage as on stage.

So I joined the Platinum Partner Program. It is a much smaller group of people who over the course of a year travel three or four times together for deep-dive seminars on specific topics. Tony and his wife Sage are the hosts, and I figured this kind of up-close format would tell me what I needed to know.

And it did. Tony and Sage are the real deal, and I was finally certain this was where I wanted to be. I applied, I was accepted, and I completed the training to be a coach. For the next five years, I just coached. And I loved it.

I would work with 65 to 85 clients at a time, in every time zone, all over the United States, Europe and Australia. People wanted help opening or improving a business, making a job change, strengthening a relationship, and other important life matters.

There was nothing in my career that equaled the excitement of being there for a light bulb moment when somebody finally sees what is possible and how to get there. It is so satisfying.

What many people do not understand about coaching is that it is not about the coach and what they know. It is what the coach can do to draw out of the clients what is in them, so they can find the insights they need.

I remember my original shock during my first coaching training at Columbia University when one of the professors said, "Take your 40 years of corporate experience and put it on the shelf. It has nothing to do with coaching." I was slack-jawed that it wasn't experience based. You had to learn to coach others, not try to hand them the answers. It wasn't about you.

Another key lesson I learned is that every coach should have a coach. When I became a Tony Robbins coach I was assigned to work with Brian Baldwin. Brian not only supported me during my five years of coaching, he was also instrumental to my success as the director of the department - but I'm getting ahead of myself.

LESSON #27: KNOW WHICH LEADERSHIP HAT YOU ARE WEARING

As a leader, the role of "coach" should be in your bag of tricks. Broadly speaking, as a leader you are always fulfilling one of the following roles:

- **Strategic thinker**: This is where you are thinking through direction. You are using your financial reports and creative thinking in this role. You are seeing what is possible and seizing opportunities.

- **Manager**: This is where you are delivering content to your team about what the plan is and making sure they know what they are doing. This is also the role of holding your direct reports accountable for the results they are producing (or not producing).

- **Coach**: This is about aligning with someone on your team to help them come to an insight. Here you ask questions and have a dialogue bent toward discovery. It could be a tough discovery along the lines of "this position is not a fit for you." Or it could be positive where they discover they already have everything they need to take a step up except confidence. Whatever it is, if you are coaching, you are trying to help them make the discovery.

[CONTINUED >]

As a leader, it can be helpful to take a beat before doing anything and ask which of these hats you are wearing right now: Strategic thinker, manager, or coach?

If what you are doing does not fit any of these roles, are you acting like a leader? It is possible you are doing the work for someone instead of being their leader?

As I said, I did this highly satisfying work for five years, and I would have been happy to do it until I retired. In fact, that is exactly what I thought would happen. But my career had one more detour.

The Director of Coaching position opened up with Tony's organization. As happy as I had been as a coach, there were things along the way I noticed that I thought could be made even better.

It was all part of acting "as-if." I had five years of viewing things from a coach's perspective and I had generated many ideas for what I thought could be done differently and better. Still, I hesitated because of how satisfied I was with coaching clients.

What finally made me throw my hat into the ring was when I got someone else to agree to get in the canoe and help me paddle. It was coach extraordinaire Brenda Schinke who had originally tapped me on the shoulder and said, "With your corporate experience, I think you should apply." I finally said I would, but told her I would need her as my #2, as Head of Coach Development. She said yes.

I wish for every leader as wonderful a working relationship as Brenda and I had. We used to jokingly call each other Lucy and Ethel after the famous friendship on the old TV show, "I Love Lucy." I will be forever grateful for her tap on the shoulder and invitation to apply for the director role. Working with Brenda has been the highlight of my 50-year career.

We made changes that deepened the relationships between coaches and their clients. We also got more specific on what "good" looks like when it comes to coaching outcomes.

The benchmarks we created allowed us to apply Lesson #11, Make Feedback Specific and Objective. It was answering the question, "How do we measure good?" By getting clear on measurements, we were able to significantly improve results in the coaching department.

LESSON #28: USE WHAT YOU LEARN...IT WORKS!

One of the great joys of my life was being able to finish my career as Director of Coaching for Robbins Research International. It became a capstone to my career. Sure, it was nice having the title and respect that went along with it. But that is not what made it such a satisfying end to my life in business.

What made it special is it brought together a lifetime of lessons and skills and put it in the service of coaching, which is something I fell in love with in the last decade of my career.

To be genuinely happy and satisfied, you cannot just have lessons in your head. You cannot just sit there with a bunch of wisdom inside you.

You have got to find ways to use it. The only way to profit from these lessons is to implement them and see how they work for you. Make some mistakes along the way, learn from them, and keep going.

As we journey into the final chapter and conclusion, that is my hope for you. That you will not just read these lessons and think "that's nice." But that you will go out and use these lessons and make them your own.

CHAPTER 19

BRINGING IT ALL TOGETHER

Often the wisdom in books remains trapped inside as soon as you close the cover. We read and learn, but then when we are faced with a challenge, we don't always recall the lessons and apply them when we need them.

My hope for this chapter is that it will serve as a handy reference when you are struggling with something, or just need some inspiration. I hope you will pull this book down off your shelf (or pull it up on your eBook reader) and open to this chapter.

HOW TO USE THIS CHAPTER

First, there is a listing of the 28 lessons in this book and what page you can find them on. Browsing them may spark your memory and interest and you can go directly to them for a brush up.

Next, there are lists of lessons broken out by category. For example, one of the categories is called Career Development. If you are struggling with a lack of advancement or have lost the plot of your career, go to that list and look at the lessons and find one or more that can help you get unstuck.

Whatever issue you are having, these groupings by topic should help you *find the answers you need when you need them.* And for one final dose of wisdom, read the conclusion that follows.

ALL 28 LESSONS

Note: On the topic lists that follow, some lessons appear in more than one category, because these lessons have multiple applications.

LESSONS FOR CAREER DEVELOPMENT

LESSONS FOR IMPROVING COMMUNICATION

LESSONS FOR BATTLING THROUGH ADVERSITY

CONCLUSION

I would like to end with a thought from Tony Robbins' book *Unshakeable: Your Financial Freedom Playbook*. As the subtitle indicates, it is mostly about personal finance and investment. However, Tony also puts some serious wisdom in Chapter 9, "Real Wealth: Making the Most Important Decision of Your Life."

From that chapter:

"**A Beautiful State**. When you feel love, joy, gratitude, awe, playfulness, ease, creativity, drive, caring, growth, curiosity, or appreciation, you're in a beautiful state…

A Suffering State. When you're feeling stressed out, worried, frustrated, angry, depressed, irritable, overwhelmed, resentful, or fearful, you're in a suffering state…

So what determines whether you're in a beautiful state or a suffering state? You might assume that it depends mostly on your external circumstances. If you're relaxing on the beach and eating ice cream, it's easy to be in a beautiful state! *But in reality, the mental and emotional state in which you live is ultimately the result of where you choose to focus your thoughts.*"

This quote gets to the heart of so many of the lessons in this book. We are always choosing between a beautiful state or a suffering state. Those states are determined by what we focus on, and our focus is generated by the questions we ask ourselves and others.

- We can be a victim… or we can "be the board."

- We can make ourselves miserable by judging our neighbor… or we can figure out our own role in the situation.

- We can wallow in our failures… or we can realize that we only fail when we fail to learn.

- We can say there is nothing good about this circumstance… or we can keep asking questions until we find something great about the situation.

Every instant you have the choice to be in a beautiful state or to suffer. Make your decision.

And one final thought after a lifetime in business: Life is a grand adventure. Treat it as such.

APPENDIX 1: HIRING A COACH

I believe hiring a coach can be a game-changer. I know it was for me, and I know the massive impact it had for many of my clients.

What makes coaching so powerful is that coaches are an outside observer who can see what you cannot. Think of personal development coaching like athletic coaching. Athletes cannot see their own technique. They need a coach to see it and correct it.

A team can't see that the same play is beating them every time, they need a coach to observe the overall pattern and point out what is going on. The athlete is in the moment, and having that objective observer makes a big difference.

Personal and business development coaching works the same way. Just like an athletic coach who stands on the sidelines and watches, a personal coach stands and listens to your hopes, dreams, and goals. Coaches pick up on things like speech patterns, how you talk about success and failure, and how you describe interacting with others. They can then illuminate the holes in your thinking. They can see what patterns are holding you back.

Coaches are an accountability partner, but they are much more than that if they are trained and good at what they do. They will pick up on your blind spots. Invest in a coach, particularly if you are feeling stuck. A coach also holds you to a higher standard than you will ever hold for yourself.

You do need to be careful when selecting one. The word "coach" has become such a popular term that now teachers, therapists, and consultants use it to describe what they do. They may be helpful in their area of expertise, but true coaches will be trained to help you make your own discoveries with skillful questions.

How do you find a good coach, one you can trust? First, figure out how they were trained and something about the organization that trained them. There are some "coaches" who got their "certification" at a weekend seminar at a beach hotel.

I can of course be accused of bias, but what I am about to say comes comes from my own experience. I recommend Robbins coaches without hesitation because of the training and quality control.

Whether you choose Robbins or some other avenue, coaching can be a game-changer. Do your due diligence and find the right one.

APPENDIX 2:
RECOMMENDED BOOKS

The Art of Possibility: Transforming Professional and Personal Life
by Rosamund Stone Zander and Benjamin Zander

Making Feedback Work by Elaine Holland

Conversations for Action and Collected Essays by Fernando Flores,
edited by Maria Flores Letelier

The Trusted Advisor by David H. Maister, Charles H. Green, and Robert
M. Galford

Maestro: A Surprising Story About Leading by Roger Nierenberg

The Ultimate Blueprint of an Insanely Successful Business
by Keith Cunningham

The PRIMES: How Any Group Can Solve Any Problem by Chris McGoff

Loving What Is: Four Questions That Can Change Your Life
by Byron Katie

*The Road Less Traveled: A New Psychology of Love, Traditional Values and
Spiritual Growth* by M. Scott Peck

Transitions: Making Sense of Life's Changes by William Bridges

Unshakeable: Your Financial Freedom Playbook by Tony Robbins
(especially Chapter 9)

ACKNOWLEDGMENTS

This book would not have been possible without Dave Moffitt's support and guidance. Dave's conversational style helped me recall the high and low points of my career and pull the insights and lessons into this book. I also owe a special thanks to Bruce Trachtenberg whose superb copyediting skills have helped make this book better and easier to read.

I am also grateful to those who took a chance on me during my 50-year career. Special thanks to Dave O'Keeffe, Tom Jenkins, Chappie Maxwell, Humphrey Penney, John King and Tony Robbins.

And a heartfelt thanks to the FOBs or Friends of Barbara; Kate, Janet, Marjorie, Tricia, and Barbara G. The loss of our mutual friend, Barbara Riefle brought us together. You have been an invaluable source of support, celebration, and learning over the decades.

www.ingramcontent.com/pod-product-compliance
Lightning Source LLC
Chambersburg PA
CBHW060427130626
46555CB00005B/2254